PRESCRIPTION FOR THE IMPOTENT CHRISTIAN

by T. A. Conway, M. D.

Copyright © 2002 by T. A. Conway, M. D.

A Prescription for the Impotent Christian
by T. A. Conway, M. D.

Printed in the United States of America

Library of Congress Control Number: 2002114375
ISBN 1-591602-91-2

All rights reserved. No part of this publication may be reproduced or transmitted in any form or by any means without written permission of the publisher.

Unless otherwise indicated, Bible quotations are taken from the New International Version. Copyright © 1985 by The Zondervan Corporation.

Xulon Press
11350 Random Hills Road
Suite 800
Fairfax, VA 22030
(703) 279-6511
XulonPress.com

To order additional copies, call 1-866-909-BOOK (2665).

This Book Is Dedicated To:

…to Him who is able to do immeasurably more than all we ask or imagine, according to his power that is at work within us, to Him be glory in the church and in Christ Jesus throughout all generations, for ever and ever! Amen. **Ephesians 3:20-21 (NIV)**

TABLE OF CONTENTS

Introduction 9

Chapter 1: The Instantaneous Transformation 11

Chapter 2: The Ineffective Christian 29

Chapter 3: Paul's Mystery 49

Chapter 4: Entering God's Workshop 67

Chapter 5: I Hate That Word "Discipline" 81

Chapter 6: Slow and Steady 111

Chapter 7: Am I Perfect Yet 141

INTRODUCTION

The book that you now hold in your hand is a simple act of obedience to God. I don't claim to be an author and I know what you're thinking, "Not another spiritual book!" Yes, it is. Is this book different from all the others? Is it going to change your life? Only God knows the answer to that. I do know, however, that it is not by accident that it sits before you. I pray that God will use it to open your eyes so that you can live a fulfilled, joyful life—the life that God intended for you. Don't think for a second that just because I've written this book it means that I have "arrived." I can assure you that I am just beginning to fathom the love that God has for me. I've spent 25 years muddling through my life trying to put together "the big picture." God has taught me some difficult lessons through the years. It's true, He has blessed me abundantly, but I have to admit that I've struggled with insecurity, addictions, and many other problems, which, *in spite of my determination*, I could never seem to get a handle on. I cried out for help, but I never seemed to be able to change—at least not for very long. Are you tired of being unproductive in your Christian life? Would you like to understand what Jesus meant when he said

A Prescription for the Impotent Christian

Matthew 11:28-30 (NIV)
"Come to me, all you who are weary and burdened, and I will give you rest. Take my yoke upon you and learn from me, for I am gentle and humble in heart, and you will find rest for your souls. For my yoke is easy and my burden is light."

America is full of "lukewarm", impotent Christians. What did Jesus say about those who were "lukewarm?"

Revelation 3:14-20 (NIV)
These are the words of the Amen, the faithful and true witness, the ruler of God's creation. I know your deeds, that you are neither cold nor hot. I wish you were either one or the other! So, because you are lukewarm—neither hot nor cold—I am about to spit you out of my mouth. You say, 'I am rich; I have acquired wealth and do not need a thing.' But you do not realize that you are wretched, pitiful, poor, blind and naked. I counsel you to buy from me gold refined in the fire, so you can become rich; and white clothes to wear, so you can cover your shameful nakedness; and salve to put on your eyes, so you can see. Those whom I love I rebuke and discipline. So be earnest, and repent. Here I am! I stand at the door and knock. If anyone hears my voice and opens the door, I will come in and eat with him, and he with me.

I don't know about you, but I'm ready for more. Read on and I promise you that God will teach you some things. I'll share with you what I believe is the "prescription" for the impotent Christian.

T. A. Conway, M.D.

— Chapter 1 —

THE INSTANTANEOUS TRANSFORMATION

On September 11th, 2001, the United States of America was shocked by the World Trade Center terrorist attack. Since that time we've seen an array of emotions. Our country has been reintroduced to words that many thought had been forgotten: God, prayer, patriotism, and heroism. America saw the face of evil and realized that there *is* a battle raging between good and evil. It has caused a *restlessness* in many human souls and many are searching for a little hope—some "good news." I am happy to report that there is some "good news." There is an answer for a restless heart in this very troubled world. What is this "good news" and how does it apply to you and me?

Let's first develop a foundation on which to build. I know it's a big step for some, but let's assume that there is a God in Heaven and that He cares about each and every individual on this planet. The Bible is His message, His word, and we can trust what He says in it. This book is not intended to provide proof of God's existence, or to prove the infallibility of His word (the Bible). Many, over the years, have debated these issues. The volumes written could fill many libraries. So for now, just accept God at His word. Lay aside any preconceived notions that you have about Christianity or any other "religion." Throw them out! Forget about the "hypocrite" who's left you with a bad taste in your mouth. Let's get a fresh start.

How did we get into this mess? Let's go back to the Garden of Eden. God said that He created us in His image. We were created with a physical body, from the "dust" of the earth. Our physical bodies are, *literally*, composed of the elements of the earth and they are guided by our five senses. God then gave us an eternal soul—our mind, will, and emotions. The body *can't* live without the soul and if the body dies the soul departs. We were given the freedom to choose (free will). God wasn't interested in a robot; He wanted to have a loving *relationship* with his creation. Lastly, God put within Adam and Eve His Spirit. The Bible says God is Spirit.

John 4:24(NIV)
> God is spirit, and his worshipers must worship in spirit and in truth.

This was what allowed Adam and Eve to "plug into" the spiritual realm and to experience true communication with God. This represented the complete human—body, soul, and spirit. It's an interesting parallel that the complete human is like the Trinity. I believe it was no mistake that when God said in Genesis 1:26 "Let *us* make man in *our* image, in *our* likeness...." The "us" and "our" referred to the Holy Trinity—Father, Son, and Holy Spirit.

God placed Adam and Eve in a perfect environment (with their free will functioning) and asked that they not do one thing; eat from a certain tree in the garden. They, however, choose to disobey God and with this disobedience came consequences. God had told them that if they ate from that certain tree they would surely "die." This meant not only the eventual death of the physical body, but, more importantly, the immediate death, or removal, of the spirit within them. Oh what a "fall" it was! Kicked out of the garden and now no ability to interact with God on a personal level. They were now separated from God and the barriers seemed too large to overcome. Mankind has tried to remove the barriers time and time again throughout history. This is the definition of "religion." We try in our *own* power and might to break down these barriers through certain rituals, lifestyles, or other activities. We're trying to change the external man—our outer appearance and behavior. We're trying to find a way to get close to God. If you haven't noticed, all of mankind's efforts to reach God always come up short. It will *always,* eventually, leave you empty—wanting more, never complete. You might find something that seems to temporarily satisfy, but sooner or later it will quit working. If we can't overcome the barriers on our own, what can we do to break them down? **It's not about what *we* can do, but about what God has** *already done.*

We've been talking about separation and barriers but what exactly do we mean? Let's discuss the barriers now. You will then have a much better idea of how far we really are from God. God (Father, Son, and Holy Spirit) has a *perfect character*—there are ten absolute attributes of God's character. Take a look at the following chart:

A Prescription for the Impotent Christian

GOD

SOVEREIGN (PERFECT WILL)	**OMNICIENT** (ALL KNOWING)
RIGHTEOUS (PERFECT STANDARD)	**OMNIPRESENT** (EVERYWHERE)
JUST (TOTALLY FAIR)	**OMNIPOTENT** (ALL POWERFUL)
LOVE (INFINITE, AGAPE)	**IMMUTABLE** (NEVER CHANGES)
ETERNAL LIFE (ALWAYS EXISTED)	**VERACITY** (ABSOLUTE TRUTH)

(HOLY SPIRIT) (SON) (FATHER)

The Instantaneous Transformation

If you want to be in God's presence, or to have fellowship with Him, you need to be *perfect* in character as He is. You need to possess *every* attribute that God possesses. Look at that chart again! Do you think you can do it? An even better question is, "Have you done it?" If not, then even one "slip-up" will separate you from God. Remember there's no room for error. Matthew 5:48 says "Be *perfect*, therefore, as your heavenly Father is perfect." What else does the Bible say?

Rom. 3:10-12 (NIV)
As it is written: "There is *no one righteous, not even one*; there is no one who understands, no one who seeks God. All have turned away, they have together become worthless; there is no one who does good, not even one.

Rom. 3:23 (NIV)
....for all have sinned and fall short of the glory of God

It's very clear—God has a high standard and we fail to measure up. This is an area where many people get confused—some even arrogant and prideful. They think in their heart, "I'm not that bad of a person", but it's not about how good you have been, or can be. The point is that you can't be *good enough*—it's an unreachable goal! It doesn't matter whether you go to church every Sunday, give money to the poor, or have been baptized and confirmed. It's not about "good deeds." What does the Bible say about our "good deeds?"

Isaiah 64:6-7 (NIV)
All of us have become like one who is unclean, and *all our righteous acts are like filthy rags*; we all

shrivel up like a leaf, and like the wind our sins sweep us away. No one calls on your name or strives to lay hold of you; for you have hidden your face from us and made us waste away because of our sins.

Does God have a "righteousness scale" that at the end of your life weighs your deeds? If the "good" outweighs the "bad" then you make it into Heaven—whew, that was close! I don't think so. God demands that you be *perfect* in character before He will accept you. Not perfect? No Heaven.

Discouraged yet? Hold tight the story is beginning to unfold. It's easy to be discouraged at this point and that's all right. The Bible says in 1 Peter 5:5 that "God opposes the proud but gives grace to the humble." Jesus had harsh words for the Pharisees, the "religious" snobs of that day. He gave us an interesting parable in Luke's gospel. Read what He said:

Luke 18:9-14 (NIV)
To some who were confident of their own righteousness and looked down on everybody else, Jesus told this parable: "Two men went up to the temple to pray, one a Pharisee and the other a tax collector. The Pharisee stood up and prayed about himself: 'God, I thank you that I am not like other men—robbers, evildoers, adulterers—or even like this tax collector. I fast twice a week and give a tenth of all I get.' "But the tax collector stood at a distance. He would not even look up to heaven, but beat his breast and said, 'God, have mercy on me, a sinner.' "I tell you that this man, rather than the other, went home justified before God. For everyone who exalts himself will be humbled, and he who humbles himself will be exalted."

The Instantaneous Transformation

The Pharisees thought they were *righteous* and *acceptable* to God, because of their outward life, their external behavior, but it's always been the "sinner" who *humbles* himself and cries out for God's mercy that finds favor with God. Why? Because they've finally reached a point where they realize they will *never* measure up to God's standard.

Now that you understand that you need to be perfect, what about all the "slip-ups" that happened *before* your "new-found" knowledge? This would be another barrier—actually, an extension of the first. We all have a *debt of sin*—this includes the past, present, and future sins of everyone in the world that has ever been born. They need to be dealt with—washed away—before anyone can see, or be with, God. I don't think this is difficult to understand. Our history is jammed with examples of unspeakable evil that has been perpetrated on mankind by other human beings. Don't forget, however, that we *all* contribute to this debt of sin. It's not about "big sins" or "little sins." In God's economy, *sin is sin*, and all of it is repulsive and unacceptable to Him.

Are there still more barriers? I'm afraid so. The next barrier deals with whom we are born to serve—it involves our "birthright." This one can be a little confusing, but I believe it's important to understand, especially in light of what we're seeing in the world at this very hour. It concerns what other human beings are doing in the name of god. Yes, I purposely used a lower case "g" because I'm talking about the "god of this world"—the Apostle Paul talked about him in the following verse:

2 Corinthians 4:4(NIV)
The *god* of this age has blinded the minds of unbelievers, so that they cannot see the light of the gospel of the glory of Christ, who is the image of God.

Here are some other verses to make the point:

Ephesians. 2:1-3(NIV)
As for you, you were dead in your transgressions and sins, in which you used to live *when you followed the ways of this world and of the ruler of the kingdom of the air, the spirit who is now at work in those who are disobedient.* All of us also lived among them at one time, gratifying the cravings of our sinful nature and following its desires and thoughts. Like the rest, we were by nature objects of wrath.

1 John 5:19(NIV)
We know that we are children of God, and that the whole world is under the control of the evil one.

Many fail to understand that mankind had been given dominion (control) over the earth at the beginning of creation (see Genesis 1:28) and after the "fall" there was a *legal transfer* of control over to Satan. Now, Satan had become the *master* of all men who would ever be born into this world. We, in effect, are all born as his "slaves." Satan took control of our planet and everything on it. Read what Satan said to Jesus.

Luke 4:5-8(NIV)
The devil led him up to a high place and showed him in an instant all the kingdoms of the world. And he said to him, "I will give you all their authority and splendor, *for it has been given to me, and I can give it to anyone I want to.* So if you worship me, it will all be yours." Jesus answered, "It is written: 'Worship the Lord your God and serve him only.'"

The Instantaneous Transformation

Satan couldn't have offered it to Jesus unless it was already his!

So, not only can we not meet God's character standard, we have a debt of sin and are "slaves" to Satan, who is at present, in control of the world. Don't think for a second that this means Satan is more powerful than God; God is still sovereign (remember the attribute chart) and He is *ultimately* in control. God just has a knack of taking Satan's, so-called, victories and turning them into situations that glorify Himself. It's easier now to understand why the terrorists act the way they do—they are serving their god, Satan. Whom we serve will be made known by our actions (deeds). Satan's goals in this world have always been to steal, kill, and destroy (see John 10:10). I think it's very evident whom the terrorists are serving—their deeds give them away.

1 Peter. 5:8(NIV)
Be self-controlled and alert. Your enemy the devil prowls around like a roaring lion looking for someone to devour.

Satan will continue to use humans for his purposes and then discard them. He hates everything about God and you, and wants nothing more than to have you believe that he doesn't exist—that he is a *fairy tale*. I think that America has been awakened to the fact that evil does exist and we have seen it's (his) face. The question is, "How can we remove this barrier and no longer serve the god of this world?" This is also an impossible barrier to overcome on our own because it's our "birthright." Satan is our father by birth and we will *naturally* follow after him until this is changed.

The last barrier to discuss was briefly mentioned earlier in the chapter. It has to do with the *death of our Spirit*. Remember that Adam and Eve were given God's Spirit—that special ability to relate to, and communicate with, God.

This dimension is what made us like God because God says He is Spirit.

John 4:23-24(NIV)
> Yet a time is coming and has now come when the true worshipers will worship the Father in spirit and truth, for they are the kind of worshipers the Father seeks. *God is spirit,* and his worshipers must worship in spirit and in truth.

Because of the spiritual death in the beginning, mankind is missing this dimension and *until we get it back we will be unable to have a relationship with God.* How can we retrieve God's Spirit? This, as you can imagine, is like all of the others—an impossible barrier to overcome. Are you tired of talking about all the barriers? Do you feel a little distant from God?

It's time to switch our focus. We now understand that there exists an enormous gap, a separation, between God and man and He seems inaccessible. Don't forget, however, that one of His character traits is that He is *all knowing* (omniscient). He knew that none of us would ever be able to have a relationship with Him *ever again* unless He did something to remedy this situation. He had to take matters, literally, into his own hands. He chose to put on a human body and come into this mixed up world to fix the problems that existed between He and His creation. Why? Because He loved us. I think almost everyone knows John 3:16: **"For God so loved the world that he gave his one and only Son, that whoever believes in him shall not perish but have eternal life."**

Jesus said in John 15:13 (NIV) "Greater love has no one than this, that he lay down his life for his friends."

What about this Jesus? I think most will agree that He did exist in history. I am now asking you to take it a little fur-

The Instantaneous Transformation

ther. Jesus asked his disciples in Mark 8:29 (NIV). "Who do you say that I am?" He is ultimately asking every one of us the same question. Not only will each of us have to answer this question, but we will need to answer the question—"What will you do with this Jesus?"

C. S. Lewis, the brilliant British scholar, said of Jesus in his book, *Mere Christianity:*

> **"I'm trying here to prevent anyone saying the really foolish thing that people often say about Jesus: `I'm ready to accept Jesus as a great moral teacher, but I don't accept His claim to be God.' That is the one thing we must not say. A man who was merely a man and said the sort of things Jesus said would not be a great moral teacher. He would either be a lunatic-on the level with the man who says he is a poached egg—or else he would be the Devil of Hell. You must make your choice. Either this man was, and is, the Son of God, or else a madman or something worse. You can shut Him up for a fool, you can spit at Him and kill Him as a demon, or you can fall at His feet and call Him Lord and God. But let us not come up with any patronizing nonsense about His being just a great human teacher. He has not left that open to us. He did not intend to."** '

C. S. Lewis, *Mere Christianity* (New York: The Macmillan Company, 1943).

I believe that *both* the Old and New Testament make it exceptionally clear that Jesus was God, in the flesh. There are a multitude of verses which state that He came from God, and actually was God. He accepted worship, performed miracles, and forgave sins. The Old Testament has over three hundred prophetic passages about the first coming of Jesus and all were fulfilled perfectly by His life on earth. Some of these prophecies were very detailed and specific. The probability of this great number of predictions being fulfilled, *by chance*, in the life of one man, is staggering. It would make your odds of winning the lottery look promising.

Understand this carefully; there is *no other name* under heaven by which man can be saved. Jesus is the key by which we gain entrance through the door of heaven. This is not about "religion" it's about the person of Jesus Christ. I realize that this view is not "politically correct" and many criticize this view as being too "narrow-minded", but after seeing how large the barriers are to overcome, God's plan makes perfect sense—after all, *He's* done all the work.

John 14:6-7(NIV)
> Jesus answered, "I am the way and the truth and the life. No one comes to the Father except through me. If you really knew me, you would know my Father as well. From now on, you do know him and have seen him."

Jesus was born of a virgin (without a human father) in order that He would not have the "birth right" that we talked about earlier. The first Adam was created without a "sin nature" and so was Jesus (the second Adam). Jesus lived a perfect, sinless life. It was a life that satisfied God's exact requirements. Jesus then went *voluntarily* to the cross and experienced intense suffering, shame, and ultimately both physical and spiritual death on that cross. God made it clear in the following verse that without the "shedding of blood" there is no remission of sin.

Hebrews 9:22(NIV)
In fact, the law requires that nearly everything be cleansed with blood, and without the *shedding of blood* there is no forgiveness.

God placed upon Jesus the collective sins of the *entire world*—past, present, and future. This included yours and mine. God, the Father, then turned away—He couldn't look upon this sin because of His perfect character. Jesus experienced spiritual death (separation) and cried out "My God, my God, why have you forsaken me?"(Matthew 27:46). He then experienced physical death. Notice that pattern was just like it was in the Garden of Eden, Adam and Eve, after their disobedience, experienced separation from God and spiritual death. Later came the physical death. God temporarily covered Adam and Eve's nakedness with the skin from an animal (maybe a lamb?). This innocent animal had to die in order to give up its skin. Remember, without the "shedding of blood" there is no forgiveness of sin. They tried to cover themselves with fig leaves. This was man's first attempt at "religion." They were trying to cover their "nakedness" and disgrace. It was God, however, who provided the *temporary* covering and knew that He would ultimately, a little later in history, provide the permanent cure by sacrificing his own son (the Lamb of God who takes away the sin of the world- see John 1:29).

After dying, Jesus was placed in a tomb and, on the third day, was bodily resurrected. This is another feature of *true* Christianity. It is not present in any other human "religion." Mohammed is still dead, as is Confucius, Buddha, and all the others. I would challenge anyone to examine the circumstantial evidence surrounding the issue of Jesus' resurrection. There is little doubt that it occurred and that He is alive today. Jesus appeared to His followers after His resurrection many times. They touched Him, ate joyed His company, until forty days later ascended bodily into Heaven before their remember how the apostles were behaving after the crucifixion? They were hiding out, depressed. They didn't know what to do next! Ultimately, most of them were tortured and died as martyrs for their Lord. Is this something you would have done if you knew, in your heart, that Jesus was really still dead and that you had helped to steal and hide his body to perpetuate a lie? I don't think so. It would have ended right then, or shortly thereafter.

We saw that sin erected large barriers between God and man, and it's only through Christ's death and resurrection that these barriers are removed. On the cross, Jesus *satisfied* God's offended character. He paid the sin debt of each and every person that has ever lived and died, "spiritually" and "physically", *in our place.* Not only did He make it possible to remove our sin, He made it possible to add His righteousness to us.

2 Corinthians 5:21 (NIV)
God made him who had no sin to be sin for us, so that in him we might become the righteousness of God.

This "righteousness" is *free* and *totally complete*. It is a "gift"—given to anyone who will simply ask for it. Once received, it cannot be added to, improved upon, or taken away.

We've touched upon the breaking down of barriers: the removal of sin *and* the addition of righteousness. What about the spiritual death that we talked about earlier? Can we recover this? Can our Spirit be reborn? This is a good time to listen in on a conversation that Jesus had with

The Instantaneous Transformation

Nicodemus, a respected religious leader of the time. Nicodemus knew his "religion." Read this carefully.

> **John 3:1-21 (NIV)**
> Now there was a man of the Pharisees named Nicodemus, a member of the Jewish ruling council. He came to Jesus at night and said, "Rabbi, we know you are a teacher who has come from God. For no one could perform the miraculous signs you are doing if God were not with him." In reply Jesus declared, "I tell you the truth, no one can see the kingdom of God unless he is born again." "How can a man be born when he is old?" Nicodemus asked. "Surely he cannot enter a second time into his mother's womb to be born!" Jesus answered, "I tell you the truth, no one can enter the kingdom of God unless he is born of water and the Spirit. Flesh gives birth to flesh, but the Spirit gives birth to spirit. You should not be surprised at my saying, 'You must be born again.' The wind blows wherever it pleases. You hear its sound, but you cannot tell where it comes from or where it is going. So it is with everyone born of the Spirit." "How can this be?" Nicodemus asked. "You are Israel's teacher," said Jesus, "and do you not understand these things? I tell you the truth, we speak of what we know, and we testify to what we have seen, but still you people do not accept our testimony. I have spoken to you of earthly things and you do not believe; how then will you believe if I speak of heavenly things? No one has ever gone into heaven except the one who came from heaven—the Son of Man. Just as Moses lifted up the snake in the desert, so the Son of Man must be lifted up, that everyone who believes in him may

have eternal life. "For God so loved the world that he gave his one and only Son, that whoever believes in him shall not perish but have eternal life. For God did not send his Son into the world to condemn the world, but to save the world through him. Whoever believes in him is not condemned, but whoever does not believe stands condemned already because he has not believed in the name of God's one and only Son. This is the verdict: Light has come into the world, but men loved darkness instead of light because their deeds were evil. Everyone who does evil hates the light, and will not come into the light for fear that his deeds will be exposed. But whoever lives by the truth comes into the light, so that it may be seen plainly that what he has done has been done through God."

This is what Jesus was talking about—no one will be with God unless they are "born again" spiritually. You need to have the Spirit added back to your physical body and soul. *This is the only thing that will complete you as a human being.* How do you get it back? This is the easy part—remember, God did all the work—He asks only one thing of us—that we accept, *by faith,* what He has already done for us.

What is "faith?"

Heb. 11:1 (NIV)
   Now faith is being sure of what we hope for and certain of what we do not see.

All He asks is that you believe that He sent his Son, Jesus, to die in your place–to remove your sin. Then accept (receive) Jesus' righteousness as your own, and ask His Holy Spirit to come into your life. This is the rebirth of the Spirit.

Notice that we're required to do more than just believe. Look at what James said about just believing in God:

James 2:19(NIV)
You believe that there is one God. Good! Even the demons believe that—and shudder.

The key is to receive it as your own. Take it—It's *your* "*gift.*" Read what the Apostle Paul said to sum it all up.

Ephesians 2:8-9(NIV)
For it is by grace you have been saved, through faith—and this not from yourselves, it is the *gift of God*—not by works, so that no one can boast.

What is "grace?" It's defined as unmerited favor. Getting something free that you don't deserve. Hal Lindsay, a gifted evangelist and teacher, had this acronym in his book, "Amazing Grace": **G**od's **R**iches **A**t **C**hrist's **E**xpense.

Years ago an anonymous writer summed up the extraordinary influence, and impact, that the life of Jesus of Nazareth had produced on mankind.

One Solitary Life

He was born in an obscure village, the child of a peasant woman. Until He was thirty, He worked in a carpenter shop and then for three years He was an itinerant preacher. He wrote no books. He held no office. He never owned a home. He was never in a big city. He never traveled two hundred miles from the place He was born. He never did any of the things that usually accompany greatness. The authorities condemned His teachings. His friends deserted Him. One betrayed Him to His enemies

for a paltry sum. One denied Him. He went through the mockery of a trial. He was nailed upon a cross between two thieves. While He was dying, His executioners gambled for the only piece of property He owned on earth: His coat. When He was dead He was taken down and laid in a borrowed grave. Nineteen centuries have come and gone, yet today He is the crowning glory of the human race, the adored leader of hundreds of millions of the earth's inhabitants. All the armies that ever marched and all the navies that were ever built and all the parliaments that ever sat and all the rulers that ever reigned - put together - have not affected the life of man upon this earth so profoundly as that One Solitary Life.

What will you do with this Jesus? If you bow your heart now and tell Him that you accept His gift, He will impart to you a new life and you too can be *spiritually reborn*. This, my friends, is what I call the "instantaneous transformation." It truly is the greatest miracle of all. But wait, it's just the beginning. This brings me to the purpose of my book—where do we go from here?

— Chapter 2 —

THE INEFFECTIVE CHRISTIAN

In the first chapter, we were taken to the point of the "instantaneous transformation." It was the rebirth of the spirit—the salvation of the human soul. Don't forget, however, that this is just the beginning. Paul says that we are a "new creation" in Christ and that we are like infants.

> **2 Corinthians 5:17(NIV)**
> Therefore, if anyone is in Christ, he is a *new creation*; the old has gone, the new has come!

> **1 Corinthians 3:1-3(NIV)**
> Brothers, I could not address you as spiritual but as worldly—*mere infants in Christ*. I gave you milk, not solid food, for you were not yet ready for it. Indeed, you are still not ready. You are still worldly.

Paul also compares this new life to a race and a race always has a starting line and a finish line. What's the point? Most individuals start the race in a sprint but quickly "run out of gas." There are many good Christian ministries that present the message of the "instantaneous transformation" (salvation) quite well. The altars are filled with people making commitments to Jesus Christ, accepting the "gift" that we talked about earlier, but they fail to get the practical tools they need to grow and develop this new relationship. These "new creatures in Christ" are usually told, before they leave, to "read your Bibles, pray, and find a good church." This is, indeed, crucial information but I believe it falls woefully short of adequately addressing the problem.

Jesus told a parable that, I believe, underscores this whole issue. He uses the analogy of the seed to make His point.

Mark 4:3-20 (NIV)
"Listen! A farmer went out to sow his seed. As he was scattering the seed, some fell along the path, and the birds came and ate it up. Some fell on rocky places, where it did not have much soil. It sprang up quickly, because the soil was shallow. But when the sun came up, the plants were scorched, and they withered because they had no root. Other seed fell among thorns, which grew up and choked the plants, so that they did not bear grain. Still other seed fell on good soil. It came up, grew and produced a crop, multiplying thirty, sixty, or even a hundred times."

Then Jesus said, "He who has ears to hear, let him hear."

When he was alone, the Twelve and the others around him asked him about the parables. He told them, "The secret of the kingdom of God has been given to you. But to those on the outside everything is said in parables so that,"' they may be ever seeing but never perceiving, and ever hearing but never understanding; otherwise they might turn and be forgiven!'"

Then Jesus said to them, "Don't you understand this parable? How then will you understand any parable? The farmer sows the word. Some people are like seed along the path, where the word is sown. As soon as they hear it, Satan comes and takes away the word that was sown in them. Others, like seed sown on rocky places, hear the word and at once receive it with joy. But since they have no root, they last only a short time. When trouble or persecution comes because of the word, they quickly fall away. Still others, like seed sown among thorns, hear the word; but the worries of this life, the deceitfulness of wealth and the desires for other things come in and choke the word, making it unfruitful. Others, like seed sown on good soil, hear the word, accept it, and produce a crop—thirty, sixty or even a hundred times what was sown."

The farmer, sowing his seed, represents any person speaking God's message, His word. This word is *very powerful*.

Hebrews 4:12-13(NIV)
For the word of God is living and active. Sharper than any double-edged sword, it penetrates even to dividing soul and spirit, joints and marrow; it judges the thoughts and attitudes of the heart. Nothing in all creation is hidden from God's sight. Everything is uncovered and laid bare before the eyes of him to whom we must give account.

Isaiah 55:11(NIV)
.... So is my *word* that goes out from my mouth: It will not return to me empty, but will accomplish what I desire and achieve the purpose for which I sent it.

2 Timothy 3:16-17 (NIV)
All Scripture is God-breathed and is useful for teaching, rebuking, correcting and training in righteousness, so that the man of God may be thoroughly equipped for every good work.

Jesus Christ is actually called "the Word"

John 1:1-5 (NIV)
In the beginning was *the Word*, and *the Word* was with God, and *the Word* was God. He was with God in the beginning. Through him all things were made; without him nothing was made that has been made. In him was life, and that life was the light of men. The light shines in the darkness, but the darkness has not understood it.

What happens after this seed is sown? There are four scenarios given.

Scenario A

This person hears the word but doesn't listen to the still, small voice inside that's telling them to *receive* it as their own. They "put off" making this decision. They think in their heart, "I'll accept God's 'gift' another day." Satan comes and steals the word (seed) that was sown. The importance of acting on this still, small voice cannot be emphasized enough. We may never get another opportunity.

2 Corinthians. 6:1-2 (NIV)
As God's fellow workers we urge you not to receive God's grace in vain. For he says, "In the time of my favor I heard you, and in the day of sal-

vation I helped you." I tell you, *now is the time of God's favor, now is the day of salvation.*

Luke 12:16-20(NIV)
And he told them this parable: "The ground of a certain rich man produced a good crop. He thought to himself, 'What shall I do? I have no place to store my crops.' "Then he said, 'This is what I'll do. I will tear down my barns and build bigger ones, and there I will store all my grain and my goods. And I'll say to myself, "You have plenty of good things laid up for many years. Take life easy; eat, drink and be merry."' "But God said to him, *'You fool! This very night your life will be demanded from you.* Then who will get what you have prepared for yourself?' "This is how it will be with anyone who stores up things for himself but is not rich toward God."

James 4:13-15(NIV)
Now listen, you who say, "Today or tomorrow we will go to this or that city, spend a year there, carry on business and make money." Why, you do not even know what will happen tomorrow. What is your life? *You are a mist that appears for a little while and then vanishes.* Instead, you ought to say, "If it is the Lord's will, we will live and do this or that."

That still small voice is called the Holy Spirit and should not be ignored. The person who does, however, runs the risk of committing the only "unforgivable sin"—yes, there is one "unforgivable sin."

Matthew 12:31-33 (NIV)
And so I tell you, every sin and blasphemy will be forgiven men, but the blasphemy against the Spirit will not be forgiven. Anyone who speaks a word against the Son of Man will be forgiven, but anyone who speaks against the Holy Spirit will not be forgiven, either in this age or in the age to come. Make a tree good and its fruit will be good, or make a tree bad and its fruit will be bad, for a tree is recognized by its fruit.

If a person repeatedly ignores the gentle prodding of the Holy Spirit, they will eventually become insensitive to the Word (a "hardened heart"). As you can see, this would ultimately lead to them experiencing physical death without receiving God's "gift" of salvation. This denial of the Holy Spirit is the *only* sin that God cannot forgive. Remember, Christ forgave all the other sins. They were "nailed to the cross." We will be justified, or condemned, by our decision to accept, or reject, Jesus Christ and His "gift."

Imagine for a moment that you lived your life out on this earth for seventy, maybe eighty years. You made a decent living, but were never wealthy by any stretch of the imagination. You always wanted to be financially free, able to buy and spend whatever you wanted, but financial success never came. As your life was coming to a close, it was suddenly made known to you that, at your birth, someone had deposited one million dollars into a bank account that bore your name. It had been accumulating interest for years, and had remained untouched! As you can imagine, it had grown into a large fortune. You then discovered that this money is not transferable to anyone, not even to your closest family. When you die the account is to be cleared. The money will be gone. How would you feel? How would you react? How come no one told you? Or did they, and you just didn't hear.

Would you be confused? Hurt? You would surely be disappointed that you lost out on such a great treasure. Then, as you take your last breath, you realized it's finished—lost forever. How could everything have been different? First, you would have to have known that the money was there. Second, in order for it to be of any use to you, a withdrawal would need to be made. You would have to *receive* the money. You would have to ask for it.

Many do not realize it but there's a very similar situation for everyone on earth. The only difference is that it deals with something worth much more than any amount of money. Jesus Christ said in Matthew 16:26 (NIV) "What good will it be for a man if he gains the whole world, yet forfeits his soul? Or what can a man give in exchange for his soul?"

No amount of gold, silver, or any other riches can ever equal the value of your eternal soul. Yet, sadly, many wander through life unaware of the "gift." Even when they hear about the "gift", they never receive it as their own. If you die *unforgiven*, you can then only be judged by the deeds done while on the earth. Unfortunately, eternal separation from God (in Hell) is the *only* other option. I realize that any discussion of Hell is unpopular, but Jesus talked more about Hell than about Heaven. Why? His mission was to save anyone, and everyone, from this awful place that was originally prepared only for Satan and his demons. If you receive the "gift" as your own then your sins are washed away forever.

Psalm 103:11-12(NIV)
For as high as the heavens are above the earth, so great is his love for those who fear him; as far as the east is from the west, so far has he removed our transgressions from us.

Isaiah 43:25(NIV)
"I, even I, am he who blots out your transgressions, for my own sake, and remembers your sins no more."

Micah 7:19(NIV)
You will again have compassion on us; you will tread our sins underfoot and hurl all our iniquities into the depths of the sea.

All past, present, and future sins are gone from God's memory forever. If you have accepted Jesus offer of forgiveness, you'll never be held accountable for *any* sin. Even your *future* sins are accounted for—stop letting Satan beat you over the head with guilt about past sins. Remember that God *doesn't remember* them any more. The pressure is off! "Born-again Christians" will, however, be rewarded for good deeds done while on the earth. We've already discussed that our salvation is *complete* in Jesus Christ. We cannot add anything to it, or take anything away from it. Don't I have to do some good deeds? Recall the thief on the cross.

Luke 23:39-43(NIV)
One of the criminals who hung there hurled insults at him: "Aren't you the Christ? Save yourself and us!" But the other criminal rebuked him. "Don't you fear God," he said, "since you are under the same sentence? We are punished justly, for we are getting what our deeds deserve. But this man has done nothing wrong." Then he said, "Jesus, remember me when you come into your kingdom." Jesus answered him, "I tell you the truth, *today* you will be with me in paradise."

He didn't have any time to come down from the cross to do a few good deeds. He died beside Jesus and went to be with Him in paradise *that* day.

I've spent a little extra time on scenario "A" simply because it is the only one of the four that carries the penalty of eternal separation from God.

Let's jump ahead to Scenario D.

Scenario D

This person hears and accepts the word and experiences the "instantaneous transformation" talked about earlier.

Jesus compares this new life to a seed that sprouts and begins to grow until it produces a crop—a large, bountiful harvest. This is the other end of the spectrum—the "born-again" Christian who lives their life the way that God has intended, exhibiting the "fruit of the Spirit." What is the "fruit of the Spirit?"

Galatians 5:22-26(NIV)
> But the fruit of the Spirit is love, joy, peace, patience, kindness, goodness, faithfulness, gentleness and self-control. Against such things there is no law. Those who belong to Christ Jesus have crucified the sinful nature with its passions and desires. Since we live by the Spirit, let us keep in step with the Spirit. Let us not become conceited, provoking and envying each other.

This is every Christian's goal but, unfortunately, it's not the norm. It's my prayer that everyone who reads this book will understand where many Christians go wrong. This leads me to the other two scenarios, B and C. American Christians typically fall into one, or both, of these two scenarios.

Scenario B

The word is heard and accepted with joy. The new life begins to sprout and grow, but before it has established a big enough root system, it experiences trouble, perhaps a drought, or intense heat. Whatever the problem, it's unable to sustain itself and stops growing. It may even begin to whither and die. I have experienced this scenario in my own life.

I became a Christian in the summer between junior high and high school. I had a marvelous summer and was enjoying tremendously my new relationship with Jesus Christ. Summer ended, however, and I found myself in a frightening position when I returned to school. I knew no other Christians, other than my mother, and I quickly, because of "no root", fell away and began living like I had before. My friends initially saw a noticeable difference in my life, but I then began to experience alienation and verbal persecution from them. I was laughed at and my new nickname was "Father Todd" (I had grown up in the Catholic Church). I am ashamed to admit that I couldn't handle it and I fell away from God. Did I lose my salvation? Absolutely not! Before my "born-again experience", sin didn't really bother me; in fact sometimes it was exciting (for a while).

Proverbs 16:25(NIV)
There is a way that seems right to a man, but in the end it leads to death.

When I began to fall away from God, I was miserable. I knew I was breaking God's heart. I was no longer experiencing *fellowship* with God. Why did I feel different? I was a "new creation", and I had a new Spirit within me. The problem was that I was *grieving* this new Spirit with my behavior.

Eph. 4:30(NIV)
And do not grieve the Holy Spirit of God, with whom you were sealed for the day of redemption.

My *position* in Christ was secure—it hadn't changed—but my *experience* was something much less than God had intended. Where did I go wrong?

Keep in mind that trouble or persecution can be just about anything. For me it was "peer pressure" and an intense need for the approval of others. It could, however, be any habit, addiction, fear, or problem. Maybe a loved one gets cancer, or a good friend dies in a car accident. The list is *endless*—but the problems, whether self-inflicted or not, are real. We all bring this baggage with us when we come to Christ. That's all right, we are instructed to "come as we are." God doesn't ask that we try to clean ourselves up first. We *should* leave our problems at the foot of the cross, but in reality, most of us take the majority of our problems, and faults, with us when we leave the altar. Is this normal? Yes!

Remember, at the altar, we get Christ's *forgiveness* and He imparts upon us His *righteousness*. When God, the Father, looks at us, He sees only His son. This is how we become perfect in God eyes. This is our *true* position in Christ, but as stated before, not usually our experience. God can certainly heal, and miraculously deliver, us from any bondage, habit, or problem, *instantaneously*, but this is usually not the case. If we have a problem with pride before we go to the altar, we will very likely still have the same problem afterwards. Remember, this new life is a *beginning* and many times God chooses to take on these problems one at a time. Sometimes certain problems take years, or decades, to work through. Some of us have more than others! This "gradual transformation" is called "sanctification." It's a process of gradual change—one small step at a time. The real issue is *who* is bringing about the change. We'll have more on this later.

Scenario C

Notice that in this scenario, the word is heard and accepted and even grows, but then the surrounding thorns and weeds begin to steal nutrients, choking the plant, and the end result is no fruit. I planted a garden one-year when I was in my medical residency. Our rented home had a small backyard with massive oak trees. I planted tomato and pepper plants and boy did they take off. They grew into the most beautiful plants. They looked strong and healthy but they never developed any tomatoes or peppers. Needless to say, they were of little value. If we allow the thorns and weeds of this life to hinder our production of fruit, we will never experience the full, complete life that Jesus said we could have.

John 10:9-10(NIV)
> I am the gate; whoever enters through me will be saved. He will come in and go out, and find pasture. The thief comes only to steal and kill and destroy; *I have come that they may have life, and have it to the full.*

This, as well, is a very common scenario for the American Christian. God has blessed our country abundantly. Unfortunately, the "thorns" of this life have choked most of us. We have been caught up in the "rat race."

1 John 2:15-17(NIV)
> Do not love the world or anything in the world. If anyone loves the world, the love of the Father is

not in him. For everything in the world—the cravings of sinful man, the lust of his eyes and the boasting of what he has and does—comes not from the Father but from the world. The world and its desires pass away, but the man who does the will of God lives forever.

Materialism and consumerism run rampant in our country. The "almighty dollar" has become the premiere idol of America. Remember it's not wrong to have "things"—it's wrong to let the "things" have you.

Matt. 6:25-34(NIV)
"Therefore I tell you, do not worry about your life, what you will eat or drink; or about your body, what you will wear. Is not life more important than food, and the body more important than clothes? Look at the birds of the air; they do not sow or reap or store away in barns, and yet your heavenly Father feeds them. Are you not much more valuable than they? Who of you by worrying can add a single hour to his life? "And why do you worry about clothes? See how the lilies of the field grow. They do not labor or spin. Yet I tell you that not even Solomon in all his splendor was dressed like one of these. If that is how God clothes the grass of the field, which is here today and tomorrow is thrown into the fire, will he not much more clothe you, O you of little faith? So do not worry, saying, 'What shall we eat?' or 'What shall we drink?' or 'What shall we wear?' For the pagans run after all these things, and your heavenly Father knows that you need them. But seek first his kingdom and his righteousness, and all these things will be given to you as well. Therefore do not worry

A Prescription for the Impotent Christian

about tomorrow, for tomorrow will worry about itself. Each day has enough trouble of its own.

It's my opinion that there are too many Christians experiencing scenarios B and C. Our lives are like a roller coaster, up and down. We may have some "spiritual" success for a while, but then the troubles start. Our lives should be like the first part of a roller coaster ride. This is when the coaster gets pulled upward by a large chain. God is to be the chain of our life and, if we let Him, He will pull us up. If we stop letting Him, what happens? We fall backwards.

There are many words in Christian circles (sometimes jokingly called "Christian*ese*") to describe this phenomenon of the up and down, ineffective, Christian life. Let's discuss some of these terms. Scenario B and C Christians are sometimes called "backslidden", or "Carnal Christians." Another favorite term is "partial surrender"—this is the Christian who lets Christ into the driver's seat of his life, but then keeps reaching over, grabbing the steering wheel, and putting the car into the ditch. Jesus talked about Christians being "lukewarm." I have chosen the word "impotent" to describe many Christians. We also talk about bondage, addiction, and other "besetting" sins. *Anything* can become an addiction in our lives—food, chemicals, approval, power, money, alcohol, work, etc. One of the most damaging problems however, is the "hypocrite." The Christian whose outward life doesn't agree with what they claim to believe. In other words, the "talk" doesn't match the "walk." Sadly, many *non*-Christians use the "hypocrite" as a reason to reject Christ. Here is an interesting perspective from a wonderful evangelist, Ron Hutchcraft. I believe he captures the essence of why no one will be able to use the "hypocrite" as a reason for rejecting Christ. Please read this short story.

The Hypocrite Hang-up

Seven years of junior high band concerts. Yes, that was the special joy Karen and I shared since all three of the Hutchcraft kids were in junior high band. Now it wasn't always a supreme musical experience, but, hey, it's our kids, right? Now let's imagine you have never heard of the brilliant composer, Ludwig von Beethoven before. And I say to you, "Beethoven was a genius. His music is some of the most beautiful ever written." You're a little skeptical because you've never heard any of him, but I suggest a way to remedy that. The junior high band is having a concert this week, and they're performing Beethoven's 9th Symphony. So you go, and you come back to me saying, "I thought you said this Beethoven guy was a genius! I just heard his music - it wasn't brilliant." Now what's the problem here? It isn't Beethoven - it's the way that band played his music. Just because they don't play his music well doesn't mean the man who wrote the music wasn't a genius!

I've devoted my life to telling people about the Genius who can harmonize our lives, who wrote the music that's supposed to guide everything we do. His name is Jesus. But many people - maybe you - can't bring themselves to a point where they will put all their trust in Jesus Christ to be their own personal Savior. One of the biggest reasons? Christians! Christians who are hypocrites. Maybe some hypocrites you know have been a major roadblock in your considering Christ. Jesus clarifies what, and Who, is THE issue in this whole Christian thing. ***Mark 2:14, "As Jesus walked along, he saw Levi . . . sitting at the tax collector's booth. 'Follow Me,' Jesus told him, and Levi got up and followed Him."***

Jesus sums up here the central decision we all have to make by issuing this clear, two-word invitation that He gave to many people - "Follow Me." Jesus said, "I'm the issue. Make your decision about ME." He repeated that

A Prescription for the Impotent Christian

invitation so many times and when He was here on earth. And it's His invitation to you and me today. As for those Christians who aren't a very good advertisement - well, they're like that junior high band trying to play that Beethoven symphony. Unfortunately, some of us don't play Jesus' music very well. But that has nothing to do with Jesus. He is still the Genius who forgives our failures and loves us with "never leave you" love, and takes us to heaven when we die.

Jesus didn't say, "Follow My followers," or "follow my leaders," or "follow My religion." He said, "Follow ME." The only reason not to be a Christian is if you've got something against Jesus. And there wasn't a trace of hypocrisy in Him.

All that will matter when you keep your appointment with God is what you did with Jesus - His one and only Son who died on the cross to pay - not for His sins - but for yours. Honestly, there is no place to hide when it comes to Jesus. Either you commit yourself to this Man who died for you - or you turn your back on Him and walk away.

It IS all about Jesus. And maybe you're ready to surrender all the baggage that has kept you from His love. It's Jesus and you, because it's Jesus you're trusting, not Christianity. Maybe you're ready to begin this relationship you were created for. Tell Him that. On Judgment Day, it'll be you and Jesus. Today it's you and Jesus. In the words of an old hymn, "What will you do with Jesus? Neutral you cannot be. For someday your heart will be asking, 'What will He do with me?'

All Christians struggle with this issue of hypocrisy. We should all try to figure out how to make our outward life match what's really in our heart. What is in your heart? This is a very important question.

Luke 6:45(NIV)
The good man brings good things out of the good stored up in his heart, and the evil man brings evil things out of the evil stored up in his heart. *For out of the overflow of his heart his mouth speaks.*

How do we change our heart? What did Paul say about *himself*?

1 Timothy 1:15-16(NIV)
Here is a trustworthy saying that deserves full acceptance: Christ Jesus came into the world to save sinners—*of whom I am the worst*. But for that very reason I was shown mercy so that in me, *the worst of sinners*, Christ Jesus might display his unlimited patience as an example for those who would believe on him and receive eternal life.

Romans 7:14-18(NIV)
We know that the law is spiritual; but I am unspiritual, sold as a slave to sin. I do not understand what I do. *For what I want to do I do not do, but what I hate I do.* And if I do what I do not want to do, I agree that the law is good. As it is, it is no longer I myself who do it, but it is sin living in me. I know that nothing good lives in me, that is, in my sinful nature. *For I have the desire to do what is good, but I cannot carry it out.*

We can try in our own strength to follow all of God's Commandments, but will we succeed? The answer is no! Paul talked about it in Colossians—he called it *"self imposed worship"*—worshiping our "will."

A Prescription for the Impotent Christian

Colossians 2:20-23(NIV)
Since you died with Christ to the basic principles of this world, why, as though you still belonged to it, do you submit to its rules: "Do not handle! Do not taste! Do not touch!?" These are all destined to perish with use, because they are based on human commands and teachings. Such regulations indeed have an appearance of wisdom, with their self-imposed worship, their false humility and their harsh treatment of the body, *but they lack any value in restraining sensual indulgence.*

It's actually a form of idolatry. When you worship your own willpower. You may meet with success occasionally, but usually there will be no lasting change. Why? The change has to be an *inward* change—a change of the heart. I'll ask again—How do we change our heart?

Fortunately, this is God's department not ours. He, and His Holy Spirit, are into the "heart-changing" business. If we would let Him do His job, we could all be "scenario D" Christians.

St. Francis of Assisi said, **"Preach the gospel to all the world, and if necessary use words."**

It should be our goal to have our lives filled with God's Spirit—with His Spirit come power and might.

Zechariah 4:6(NIV)
'Not by might nor by power, *but by my Spirit,*' says the Lord Almighty.

The more we become like Christ, the more attractive our outward life will become. People will see this and they will ask, "What is it that makes you like you are? How can I have it?." Our only duty is to do as the Apostle Peter instructs us:

1 Peter 3:15-16 (NIV)
But in your hearts set apart Christ as Lord. *Always be prepared to give an answer to everyone who asks you to give the reason for the hope that you have.* But do this with gentleness and respect, keeping a clear conscience, so that those who speak maliciously against your good behavior in Christ may be ashamed of their slander.

Look at the situation that the apostles were in. They were dejected after the crucifixion. They were then undoubtedly filled with joy when they saw the resurrected Christ. They spent time with Him, intermittently, over the next forty days and then they watched him ascend bodily into Heaven. Don't you think that they were all maybe just a little excited at that moment in time—ready to tell the world about their risen Lord. But wait, what did Jesus tell them to do? He told them to wait! Wait for what? The promised Holy Spirit—which did come ten days later in Jerusalem at an event called Pentecost. Jesus knew that if they tried in their *own* power and might to preach the gospel they would be unproductive. I imagine that it was difficult for them to wait, but boy was the wait worthwhile! Peter immediately preached a message filled with the power of the Holy Spirit and three thousand were saved. There were many miracles, signs, and wonders. What was the source of the power? *The Holy Spirit.* You may be asking, "This sounds great but it doesn't seem to be happening in my life." Do you desire the same source of power in your life? What is the secret? Paul called it a *mystery*. Just what is this mystery?

1 Timothy 3:16 (NIV)
Beyond all question, the *mystery* of godliness is great: He appeared in a body, was vindicated by the Spirit, was seen by angels, was preached

among the nations, was believed on in the world, was taken up in glory.

Colossians 1:25-27(NIV)
I have become its servant by the commission God gave me to present to you the word of God in its fullness—the mystery that has been kept hidden for ages and generations, but is now disclosed to the saints. To them God has chosen to make known among the Gentiles the glorious riches of this *mystery*, which is Christ in you, the hope of glory.

The *mystery* is Jesus Christ living in you as the Holy Spirit. Remember, however, He is a perfect gentleman and will never "enter in" without an invitation.

Revelation 3:20(NIV)
Here I am! I stand at the door and knock. If anyone hears my voice and opens the door, I will come in and eat with him, and he with me.

Let's discuss this *mystery* in more detail in the next chapter.

— Chapter 3 —

Paul's Mystery

Jesus made a profound statement in the gospel of Matthew.

> **Matthew 11:28-30 (NIV)**
> "Come to me, all you who are weary and burdened, and I will give you rest. Take my yoke upon you and learn from me, for I am gentle and humble in heart, and you will find rest for your souls. *For my yoke is easy and my burden is light.*"

I have to be bluntly honest—I have never understood what Jesus meant by this statement. I could relate to weary and burdened, but I failed to understand what he meant by an *easy* yoke and a *light* burden. It certainly didn't seem easy or light to me! All those rules and regulations to follow—it seems like a pretty *hard yoke* and a *heavy burden*. Let's try to sort out what Jesus actually meant by this statement. We discussed in the first chapter that we were designed to be triune beings: body, soul, and spirit. Remember, however, that something went terribly wrong, mankind was disobedient and we died spiritually. This left us with body and soul, but *no spirit*. We all have a spiritual "hole", a void, at the center of our innermost being. It has caused a hunger in humans and we try to fill this "hole" with all sorts of things: money, power, relationships, sex, drugs, religion, etc. Nothing, however, will fit because this "hole" is "God-shaped." Only God's Spirit will fit *perfectly* and give us the "rest for our souls" that Jesus talked about.

How do humans function before they're "born-again?" We have a *body* and *soul*, but we're missing a *spirit* (the Spirit). The "body" is the physical body we're all familiar with. It communicates with the outside world via the five senses: sight, hearing, taste, touch, and smell. It's in *inseparable* communication with the "soul"—which is composed of our free will, mind, and emotions. Remember, on this earth, the soul (which is eternal) cannot exist without the body. If the body dies, the soul departs. In the center is the missing "spirit", which, as you recall, died at the fall of man. What was left? Body and soul left to their own device—now, collectively, known as the "sin nature" or the "flesh." No longer could man communicate with God—no longer could man understand "spiritual" things. We became more "self-centered." Other spirits, or spiritual things occasionally try to occupy this spiritual "hole." Don't forget there is an unseen spirit world—this includes demons and angels. We've all heard stories about spirit beings that enter into our physical world. We all know that modern science has no explanation for many of these events. Paul said that our battle was not against flesh and blood.

Ephesians 6:12 (NIV)
> For our struggle is not against flesh and blood, but against the rulers, against the authorities, against the powers of this dark world and against the spiritual forces of evil in the heavenly realms.

Satan and his demons *are very real*, but they are *spiritual* beings. They are invisible, deceitful, and exceptional actors! Jesus calls Satan a "murderer" and a "liar":

John 8:44-45 (NIV)
He (Satan) was a murderer from the beginning, not holding to the truth, for there is no truth in him. When he lies, he speaks his native language, for he is a liar and the father of lies.

2 Corinthians 11:14-15 (NIV)
And no wonder, for Satan himself masquerades as an *angel of light*. It is not surprising, then, if his servants masquerade as *servants of righteousness*. Their end will be what their actions deserve.

I believe, in certain situations, these evil spirits are allowed access into this spiritual "hole." This is the very issue of demon possession. Remember, Jesus Himself, "cast out" many demons. Here are two examples:

Luke 4:33-36 (NIV)
In the synagogue there was a man possessed by a demon, an evil spirit. He cried out at the top of his voice, "Ha! What do you want with us, Jesus of Nazareth? Have you come to destroy us? I know who you are—the Holy One of God!" "Be quiet!" Jesus said sternly. "Come out of him!" Then the demon threw the man down before them all and came out without injuring him. All the people were amazed and said to each other, "What is this teaching? With authority and power he gives orders to evil spirits and they come out!"

A Prescription for the Impotent Christian

Luke 8:27-34 (NIV)
When Jesus stepped ashore, he was met by a demon-possessed man from the town. For a long time this man had not worn clothes or lived in a house, but had lived in the tombs. When he saw Jesus, he cried out and fell at his feet, shouting at the top of his voice, "What do you want with me, Jesus, Son of the Most High God? I beg you, don't torture me!" For Jesus had commanded the evil spirit to come out of the man. Many times it had seized him, and though he was chained hand and foot and kept under guard, he had broken his chains and had been driven by the demon into solitary places. Jesus asked him, "What is your name?" "Legion," he replied, because many demons had gone into him. And they begged him repeatedly not to order them to go into the Abyss. A large herd of pigs was feeding there on the hillside. The demons begged Jesus to let them go into them, and he gave them permission. When the demons came out of the man, they went into the pigs, and the herd rushed down the steep bank into the lake and was drowned. When those tending the pigs saw what had happened, they ran off and reported this in the town and countryside.

You can see that evil spirit(s) can control a body/soul. We are seeing an explosion in interest about spiritual things. Unfortunately, much of it is not of God. Psychic hotlines, palm readers, and other "New-Age" phenomenon are all too common. What does God say about this?

Deuteronomy 18:10-13 (NIV)
Let no one be found among you who sacrifices his son or daughter in the fire, who practices divination

or sorcery, interprets omens, engages in witchcraft, or casts spells, or who is a medium or spiritist or who consults the dead. Anyone who does these things is detestable to the LORD, and because of these detestable practices the LORD your God will drive out those nations before you. You must be blameless before the LORD your God.

These are very dangerous practices to get involved in because it allows demonic spirits a way to enter into your spiritual "hole." How can this be prevented? By allowing God's Spirit to fill the "hole"—then there is no longer room for any other spirit. This is why I believe that it is not possible for any "born-again" Christian to become demon possessed. Only God's Spirit is a perfect fit! After the "instantaneous transformation" God's Spirit fills the spiritual "hole" perfectly and this opens our eyes to a new dimension. We can now truly begin to experience a relationship with God, and His son Jesus Christ. This is the reason that you can begin to read the Bible with "new eyes." You will have a new perspective.

1 Corinthians 2:10-12(NIV)

The Spirit searches all things, even the deep things of God. For who among men knows the thoughts of a man except the man's spirit within him? In the same way no one knows the thoughts of God except the Spirit of God. *We have not received the spirit of the world but the Spirit who is from God, that we may understand what God has freely given us.*

We ended the last chapter with a brief discussion of Paul's "mystery"—this "mystery" is *Christ in you*, which is God's Holy Spirit. I think we are beginning to understand

A Prescription for the Impotent Christian

our *position* in Christ but we're still struggling with our *experience*. Why can't we seem to do the right thing? Why are so many Christians struggling with all sorts of problems and addictions? If we have God's Spirit within us it should be easy—shouldn't it? There is a war that rages between the "sin nature" (flesh) and our "new nature." I think most Christians have a practical understanding of this. Our "sin nature" is a complex combination of our body and soul and includes all of our past experiences—good and bad. After our *new birth*, we are to begin our *new life* with our *new nature*—which is to be guided by God's Spirit. The problems arise when we try to live this "new life" in our *own* power. We are relying upon our old "sin nature" and this will never bring about the kind of life that pleases God. It will only cause trouble. Even worse is the situation in which people allow other spirits into their "innermost being" to get help, or find fulfillment. This was the issue of demon possession we talked about earlier.

What about God's laws? Where do they fit into the picture? What about the Ten Commandments? Isn't the Bible chocked full of all sorts of laws, rules, regulations, and recommendations? Yes it is, but what if I told you that you weren't required to follow any of them! What if I told you that you *couldn't* follow most of them even if you tried!

After Adam and Eve sinned, all that mankind had to guide them was their *conscience*—that still, small voice that everyone hears deep in their soul that says "this is right" or "this is wrong." We all have one. It wasn't long before mankind, guided by their conscience, became very evil.

Romans 1:20-21 (NIV)
For since the creation of the world God's invisible qualities—his eternal power and divine nature—have been clearly seen, being understood from what has been made, so that *men are without*

excuse. For although they knew God, they neither glorified him as God nor gave thanks to him, but their thinking became futile and their foolish hearts were darkened.

If you didn't listen to your conscience and make the "right choice", it would eventually "harden" and the natural inclination was to follow the way of Satan. You would gradually become more and more evil and rebellious toward God. Remember our earlier discussion of our "birthright" and who we are slaves to? Look at what mankind had become before the flood.

Genesis 6:5-6 (NIV)
The LORD saw how great man's wickedness on the earth had become, and that every inclination of the thoughts of his heart was only evil all the time. The LORD was grieved that he had made man on the earth, and his heart was filled with pain.

This ultimately brought about the flood and with it a fresh start. But this really did little to change the underlying problem—after the flood God still looked at a person's conscience—if they were trying to seek after Him, and follow their conscience, that was adequate. God accepted this "faith" as righteousness, *for the time*, because He knew that, a little further along in time, He would provide an answer for sin—He would redeem His creation. Remember, God is not bound by time as we are. He is eternal—without beginning and without end. It wasn't a problem for Him to do this. God did not hold anyone accountable for "sin" during this period of time. Why? Sin had not yet been defined. If there is *no law*, then God can't hold us accountable for sin.

Romans 5:12-13 (NIV)
Therefore, just as sin entered the world through one man, and death through sin, and in this way death came to all men, because all sinned—for before the law was given, sin was in the world. *But sin is not taken into account when there is no law.*

God gave "the law" to Moses on Mount Sinai—the renowned Ten Commandments. Why did God give us "the law?" God gave us "the law" to show us what sin is—to *define* sin and to make us aware of His standard.

Romans 3:19-20 (NIV)
Now we know that whatever the law says, it says to those who are under the law, so that every mouth may be silenced and the whole world held accountable to God. Therefore no one will be declared righteous in his sight by observing the law; rather, *through the law we become conscious of sin.*

Then what happened? After we were made aware of God's standard, this knowledge provoked, or aroused our "sin nature."

Romans 7:5 (NIV)
For when we were controlled by the sinful nature, *the sinful passions aroused by the law* were at work in our bodies, so that we bore fruit for death.

God could not hold anyone accountable for breaking His commandments unless He made His commandments known. Once the commandments were made known, it made breaking them even more enticing.

Most everyone is aware of the stereotype of the "preachers kid." They seem to be more rebellious than most because of this very principle. We see another example in our children—I think all parents make use of the "law of reverse psychology" in their children. Tell them not to do something in order to get them to do it. "Don't you eat that broccoli?"

What is God's ultimate purpose then for the law? To bring us to a point of hopelessness—to see that we are utterly powerless to follow all His rules—we cannot meet His standard. The natural progression should be our realization that we need a Savior. He wants us to *humbly* admit our inadequacy and helplessness. Our Savior will then rescue us from our sin and give us His Holy Spirit to empower us to live for God.

Galatians 3:24-25 (NIV)
So the law was put in charge to lead us to Christ that we might be justified by faith. Now that faith has come, we are no longer under the supervision of the law.

Hopefully you'll see that the law achieved God's purpose. **You don't have to live under any law now.** It was "nailed' to the Cross.

Colossians 2:13-15 (NIV)
When you were dead in your sins and in the uncircumcision of your sinful nature, God made you alive with Christ. *He forgave us all our sins, having canceled the written code, with its regulations, that was against us and that stood opposed to us; he took it away, nailing it to the cross.* And having disarmed the powers and authorities, he made a public spectacle of them, triumphing over them by the cross.

We are not under law but grace. We have been set free from sin.

Romans 6:11-14 (NIV)
In the same way, count yourselves dead to sin but alive to God in Christ Jesus. Therefore do not let sin reign in your mortal body so that you obey its evil desires. Do not offer the parts of your body to sin, as instruments of wickedness, but rather offer yourselves to God, as those who have been brought from death to life; and offer the parts of your body to him as instruments of righteousness. *For sin shall not be your master, because you are not under law, but under grace.*

Romans 6:22-23 (NIV)
But now that you have been set free from sin and have become slaves to God, the benefit you reap leads to holiness, and the result is eternal life. For the wages of sin is death, but the gift of God is eternal life in Christ Jesus our Lord.

If we're so free, why do we keep on struggling with sin? It has to do with this battle between the "sinful nature" and the "new nature." The Apostle Paul talked about this in some detail and the following verses provide a nice summary. This deserves a careful reading, as these are foundational truths:

Romans 7:4-25 (NIV)
So, my brothers, you also died to the law through the body of Christ, that you might belong to another, to him who was raised from the dead, in order that we might bear fruit to God. For when we were controlled by the sinful nature, the sinful

passions aroused by the law were at work in our bodies, so that we bore fruit for death. But now, by dying to what once bound us, *we have been released from the law so that we serve in the new way of the Spirit, and not in the old way of the written code.*

What shall we say, then? Is the law sin? Certainly not! Indeed *I would not have known what sin was except through the law.* For I would not have known what coveting really was if the law had not said, "Do not covet." But sin, seizing the opportunity afforded by the commandment, produced in me every kind of covetous desire. For apart from law, sin is dead. Once I was alive apart from law; but when the commandment came, sin sprang to life and I died. I found that the very commandment that was intended to bring life actually brought death. For sin, seizing the opportunity afforded by the commandment, deceived me, and through the commandment put me to death. So then, the law is holy, and the commandment is holy, righteous and good.

Did that which is good, then, become death to me? By no means! But in order that sin might be recognized as sin, it produced death in me through what was good, so that through the commandment sin might become utterly sinful.

We know that the law is spiritual; but I am unspiritual, sold as a slave to sin. I do not understand what I do. For what I want to do I do not do, but what I hate I do. And if I do what I do not want to do, I agree that the law is good. As it is, it is no longer I myself who do it, but it is sin living in me. *I know that nothing good lives in me, that is, in my sinful nature. For I have the desire to do what is*

A Prescription for the Impotent Christian

good, but I cannot carry it out. For what I do is not the good I want to do; no, the evil I do not want to do—this I keep on doing. Now if I do what I do not want to do, it is no longer I who do it, but it is sin living in me that does it.

So I find this law at work: When I want to do good, evil is right there with me. For in my inner being I delight in God's law; but I see another law at work in the members of my body, waging war against the law of my mind and making me a prisoner of the law of sin at work within my members. What a wretched man I am! Who will rescue me from this body of death? Thanks be to God—through Jesus Christ our Lord! So then, I myself in my mind am a slave to God's law, but in the sinful nature a slave to the law of sin.

The key is to harness the power of the Holy Spirit in our lives—God has *written the law upon our hearts through the Holy Spirit.*

Romans 8:1-14 (NIV)
Therefore, there is now no condemnation for those who are in Christ Jesus, because *through Christ Jesus the law of the Spirit of life set me free from the law of sin and death.* For what the law was powerless to do in that it was weakened by the sinful nature, God did by sending his own Son in the likeness of sinful man to be a sin offering. And so he condemned sin in sinful man, in order that the righteous requirements of the law might be fully met in us, who do not live according to the sinful nature but according to the Spirit.

Those who live according to the sinful nature have their minds set on what that nature desires; but those who live in accordance with the Spirit have their minds set on what the Spirit desires. The mind of sinful man is death, but the mind controlled by the Spirit is life and peace; the sinful mind is hostile to God. It does not submit to God's law, nor can it do so. Those controlled by the sinful nature cannot please God.

You, however, are controlled not by the sinful nature but by the Spirit, if the Spirit of God lives in you. And if anyone does not have the Spirit of Christ, he does not belong to Christ. But if Christ is in you, your body is dead because of sin, yet your spirit is alive because of righteousness. And if the Spirit of him who raised Jesus from the dead is living in you, he who raised Christ from the dead will also give life to your mortal bodies through his Spirit, who lives in you.

Therefore, brothers, we have an obligation—but it is not to the sinful nature, to live according to it. For if you live according to the sinful nature, you will die; but if by the Spirit you put to death the misdeeds of the body, you will live, because those who are led by the Spirit of God are sons of God.

Galatians 5:16-18 (NIV)

So I say, live by the Spirit, and you will not gratify the desires of the sinful nature. For the sinful nature desires what is contrary to the Spirit, and the Spirit what is contrary to the sinful nature. They are in conflict with each other, so that you do not do what you want. But if you are led by the Spirit, you are not under law.

What is "righteousness?" Remember from chapter one that it is a "gift" from God. At the "instantaneous transformation" we experience forgiveness of all our sin *and* we receive the impartation of Christ's righteousness. *Both* are "gifts" from God. We need to realize that this is the "easy yoke" and "light burden" that Jesus talked about. Not only will all of your sins be washed away, never to be remembered again, *He will write His law upon your heart via the Holy Spirit.* You don't have to worry about following all the rules and regulations. God didn't say there wouldn't be battles: your old "sin nature" vs. your "new nature." Remember, these two "natures" are struggling to control your body/soul. If you give God's Spirit free reign to control your "new nature" then victory is guaranteed.

So if it's a "gift" I don't have to do anything right? Will God just zap me with His "righteousness?" I think you already know the answer to this one—God will never zap you with anything you don't want. Where does the whole issue of obedience fit into this picture? It's very clear from the Bible that obedience is a very important topic:

Leviticus 18:4-5 (NIV)
You must obey my laws and be careful to follow my decrees. I am the LORD your God. Keep my decrees and laws, for the man who obeys them will live by them. I am the LORD.

John 14:23-24 (NIV)
Jesus replied, "If anyone loves me, he will obey my teaching. My Father will love him, and we will come to him and make our home with him. He who does not love me will not obey my teaching. These words you hear are not my own; they belong to the Father who sent me.

1 John 5:2-5 (NIV)
This is how we know that we love the children of God: by loving God and carrying out his commands. This is love for God: to obey his commands. And his commands are not burdensome, for everyone born of God overcomes the world. This is the victory that has overcome the world, even our faith. Who is it that overcomes the world? Only he who believes that Jesus is the Son of God.

I have to admit that I struggled with this seeming inconsistency for a long time (years). I found myself besieged with certain sins that I just couldn't seem to get under control. I knew what the Bible said about the problem and I would try *in my own strength* to overcome it. I would occasionally meet with some temporary success, but, ultimately, I would revert back to my "old" way. The problem? I was trying to make the change in my *own* strength. This will always (ultimately) fail. Do you see the paradox? God wants me to obey. I desperately want to obey, but I can't do it on my own. Only God can give me the ability to obey.

Think of it like this. You are the proud owner of a sophisticated new machine. There's only one company who makes it. This machine is running well until one day you realize something has gone wrong—it's no longer running properly. You take off the cover and look inside. You make an attempt to fix it but you realize that you're in "way over your head." There's no way you can fix it yourself. You try to find someone else to fix it, but no one is qualified. The only recourse is to take it to the manufacturer's workshop. Here they can make the necessary repairs and, before long, the machine is functioning normally again.

Does this story have a point?

You were created by a loving God who knows exactly what makes you "run." He knows we're "broken" and He desires that you come into His workshop for the necessary repairs. Please note, however, that there is a prerequisite. We first have to recognize that there is a problem. Do you know that you're "broken?" Do you realize that you're in "need of repair?" If we won't give God the time, how can we expect Him to bring about the "repairs" we long for? Are you asking God any of these questions? Why can't I stop drinking? Why do I always overeat? Why can't I control my anger? Why can't I _____ (you fill in the blank)? The list is endless. Remember, however, it takes time to make these repairs. Are you too busy to allow God the time He needs to bring the *positional* righteousness you received at the "instantaneous transformation" in alignment with the *experiential* righteousness you desire? Only then will you be able to "walk the talk."

What did Jesus say about obedience?

John 14:15 (NIV)
"*If you love me*, you will obey what I command."

Jesus never insists on our obedience. Notice that He says, "*If* you love me", meaning that we have to obey *only if it is our desire to do so*. This gets back to the topic of "free will"—it is our choice to follow after Him—to love Him. This is really all that Jesus wants—our love. He wants a relationship. If we love Him, then we should trust that if He tells us not to do something it's not because He wants us to have a boring or unfulfilled life. It's only because He doesn't want to see us get hurt. He created us and He knows how we function best. Anyone who has children will understand this concept. We tell our children not to play with knives and to stay out of the street because *we* understand the danger. Sometimes they fail to see the "big picture", and their resulting disobedience leads to harm, or worse yet, death.

No, God doesn't insist that we obey His commands, or become His servants, but after you begin to understand everything He's done for you it seems like the natural thing to do. Hal Lindsay, in his book "Amazing Grace" illustrates this truth with a wonderful story:

In the days of slavery in ancient Rome, a notorious and cruel slaveholder was in the Roman slave market to purchase some additional slaves. That particular day there was a stranger there also. He was a kindly man who was new to the market. He bought slaves in order to set them free.
A slave was put up on the dock, and the bidding started. The cruel man open the bid, and the good man immediately set forth a counter bid. The prices offers began to soar to dizzy heights as the men bid back and forth.
Finally, the good man named a price so high that the wicked slaveholder couldn't match it.
As the new owner walked up to the auctioneer of the slave market to pay the ransom, the slave marched over behind his new master and prepared to follow him.
The good man who had bought the slave turned around and said, "Your free to go. I bought you to set you free." And he started to walk away.
"Wait a minute", the slave answered. "If I'm a free man, then I'm free to follow you. My desire is to serve you out of gratitude for what you've done for me."

How can we begin to serve our Lord and Savior? How can we begin to thank Him for the "gift(s)" He has given us? He has rescued us from the unattainable demands of the law and the due penalty of our sin. We no longer need to be slaves to Satan and our "sinful natures." He has given us His own *positional* righteousness, and has filled our empty spiritual "hole" with His Holy Spirit to allow us to *experience* righteousness in our everyday life. Paul's mystery is profound:

After the "instantaneous transformation", God is living in you as the Holy Spirit. His law has been written upon your "heart" and He is ready to begin the process of the "gradual transformation." The objective: To become more and more like Jesus Christ. He is responsible for changing our "hearts" and this is the only place where *true, lasting change* can occur. Let's now enter into "God's Workshop" so that the necessary changes can begin to take place.

— Chapter 4 —

ENTERING GOD'S WORKSHOP

We should now understand that we have been given all the tools that we need to live an *effective* Christian life. At the "instantaneous transformation" we received the forgiveness of our sins and we were given the righteousness of Jesus Christ. We now realize that God's Holy Spirit (which is "Christ in you") is ready, willing, and able, to begin to make the changes that we so desire in our lives. It's time to begin the "gradual transformation"—this is a lifelong process. It is the goal of this chapter to open the door of God's workshop—so that we may enter in and begin to *allow God* to make these necessary changes.

Imagine for a moment that you're standing in the entryway, the foyer, of God's "workshop"—you desperately want to enter but, unfortunately, there is a locked door in front of you. Off to the side of the door is a built-in keypad. You are required to type in three passwords before the door will open. What might they be? Where do we start?

We briefly talked in the last chapter about recognizing that we have problems. We can't be "fixed" until we understand first that we're "broken." We can't be "healed" unless

A Prescription for the Impotent Christian

we first realize that we're "sick." Do you want to be "filled" by God's Spirit? You must first "empty" yourself. If you haven't figured it out yet, the first password is *humility*. There are many things identified in the Bible as sin, but I believe that one of the most overlooked sins is pride. It is the exact opposite of humility. Pride is very deceptive. What does God say about pride?

> **Proverbs 8:13 (NIV)**
> To fear the LORD is to hate evil; *I hate pride and arrogance*, evil behavior and perverse speech.

> **Proverbs 16:18 (NIV)**
> Pride goes before destruction, a haughty spirit before a fall.

> **Proverbs 18:12 (NIV)**
> Before his downfall a man's heart is proud, but humility comes before honor.

> **Psalm 10:4 (NIV)**
> In his pride the wicked does not seek him; in all his thoughts there is no room for God.

Wow! God hates it. It brings disgrace and destruction. It causes us to "fall." What keeps us from admitting our need for a Savior? What keeps us from confessing our sin? What keeps us from relying on God's Spirit and trying to get by in our own strength? Pride, pride, pride. As you can see, it can be a major roadblock in running our "race."

On the other hand, what does God say about humility?

> **2 Chronicles 7:14 (NIV)**
> ...if my people, who are called by my name, will humble themselves and pray and seek my face

and turn from their wicked ways, then will I *hear* from heaven and will *forgive* their sin and will *heal* their land.

Isaiah 66:2 (NIV)
Has not my hand made all these things, and so they came into being?" declares the LORD. *"This is the one I esteem*: he who is humble and contrite in spirit, and trembles at my word.

Proverbs 11:2 (NIV)
When pride comes, then comes disgrace, but *with humility comes wisdom.*

Psalm 25:9 (NIV)
He guides the humble in what is right and teaches them his way.

Psalm 149:4 (NIV)
For the LORD takes delight in his people; he crowns the humble with *salvation.*

Proverbs 22:4 (NIV)
Humility and the fear of the LORD bring *wealth and honor and life.*

God says He will *hear, forgive, and heal.* God *esteems* (admires) the humble person. He gives *salvation, wisdom, wealth, honor, and life.* I think I prefer this list to the former!

Let's examine some of the comments in the Bible regarding people God has used in powerful ways:

Numbers 12:3 (NIV)
Now Moses was a very humble man, more humble than anyone else on the face of the earth.

A Prescription for the Impotent Christian

Daniel 10:12 (NIV)
Then he continued, "Do not be afraid, Daniel. Since the first day that you set your mind to gain understanding and to humble yourself before your God, your words were heard, and I have come in response to them.

Luke 1:46-53 (NIV)
And Mary said: "My soul glorifies the Lord and my spirit rejoices in God my Savior, for he has been mindful of the humble state of his servant. From now on all generations will call me blessed, for the Mighty One has done great things for me— holy is his name. His mercy extends to those who fear him, from generation to generation. He has performed mighty deeds with his arm; he has scattered those who are proud in their inmost thoughts. He has brought down rulers from their thrones but has lifted up the humble. He has filled the hungry with good things but has sent the rich away empty.

Need I say any more about the role of Moses—we all know how mightily God used him? Notice that Daniel humbled himself *first* and then God heard and responded. Finally, God used a humble servant girl and *lifted* her up.

Let's not forget, however, the **ultimate** example of humility—Jesus Christ. I think the essence of what Jesus did is summed up in the following verse. No one "practiced what He preached" better than Jesus.

Philippians 2:3-11 (NIV)
Do nothing out of selfish ambition or vain conceit, but in humility consider others better than yourselves. Each of you should look not only to your own interests, but also to the interests of others.

> Your attitude should be the same as that of Christ Jesus: Who, being in very nature God, did not consider equality with God something to be grasped, but made himself nothing, taking the very nature of a servant, being made in human likeness. And being found in appearance as a man, he humbled himself and became obedient to death—even death on a cross! Therefore God exalted him to the highest place and gave him the name that is above every name, that at the name of Jesus every knee should bow, in heaven and on earth and under the earth, and every tongue confess that Jesus Christ is Lord, to the glory of God the Father.

Think about this for a minute. The God, who spoke the universe into existence, entered the world as an infant, grew into a man and gave Himself as a sacrifice to save his creation. He allowed Himself to be mocked, spit upon, beaten, flogged, and crucified on a wooden cross! Why? Because of His great love for you and me—to remove all those impossible barriers that we discussed before. This was *true* humility.

What did Jesus say about humility?

Matthew 23:11-12 (NIV)
> The greatest among you will be your servant. For whoever exalts himself will be humbled, and whoever humbles himself will be exalted.

Matthew 18:2-4 (NIV)
> He called a little child and had him stand among them. And he said: "I tell you the truth, unless you change and become like little children, you will never enter the kingdom of heaven. Therefore, whoever humbles himself like this child is the greatest in the kingdom of heaven.

A Prescription for the Impotent Christian

Humility is really just brokenness—when we finally realize our true position in this life. We like to think we are in control, but it takes only a second to realize just the opposite is true. Maybe a child was taken from you in a car accident, or your home was destroyed by a tornado. Think about the catastrophic events of September 11, 2001. Humility is recognizing that we are vulnerable and insufficient in ourselves. We really have no control at all! I know this makes people squirm—it's a very uncomfortable feeling. You can deny it, but the facts remain. Only *true* Christianity can give real hope, security, and peace, to your life—these are available *only* from Jesus Christ. Do you want to be filled with God's Spirit and receive the blessings that come with it? Then remember to come to God humbly. *Humility* is the first password for entering into His workshop.

James 4:6-10 (NIV)
That is why Scripture says: "God opposes the proud but gives grace to the humble." Submit yourselves, then, to God. Resist the devil, and he will flee from you. Come near to God and he will come near to you. Wash your hands, you sinners, and purify your hearts, you double-minded. Grieve, mourn and wail. Change your laughter to mourning and your joy to gloom. Humble yourselves before the Lord, and he will lift you up.

You quickly type in the word *humility*—the first of three locks opens. You now need the next password. What could it be? It also begins with the letter "H." Any ideas? Examine this verse about the Israelites when they were wandering in the desert.

Deuteronomy 8:3 (NIV)
He humbled you, causing you to hunger and then

feeding you with manna, which neither you nor your fathers had known, to teach you that man does not live on bread alone but on every word that comes from the mouth of the LORD.

How do you feel when you've gone without food for a day or two? Easy, isn't it? The second password –*hungry*! Jesus said in the following:

Matthew 5:6 (NIV)
Blessed are those who hunger and thirst for righteousness, for they will be filled.

Are you hungry for God and what He has for you? Hungry equates to *emptiness*—if you are a little hungry you can get a little of God, if you are totally empty—God can fill you up. Often we try to fill this hunger void with junk food. We take trips, overeat, and buy things to satisfy the "hunger pangs", but this is only a temporary fix and if you continue you will become severely malnourished. True satisfaction comes only when Jesus Christ fills the "God shaped hole" in your life.

Psalm 107:8-9 (NIV)
Let them give thanks to the LORD for his unfailing love and his wonderful deeds for men, for he satisfies the thirsty and fills the hungry with good things.

John 6:35 (NIV)
Then Jesus declared, "I am the bread of life. He who comes to me will never go hungry, and he who believes in me will never be thirsty.

Humility and *hunger* are the first two passwords needed to enter into God's workshop. They both very much please God.

So now, after you type in *hunger*, lock number two opens. Only one lock remains! The last password also begins with the letter "H." This verse in Hebrews will give you the answer.

Hebrews 12:10-14 (NIV)
Our fathers disciplined us for a little while as they thought best; but God disciplines us for our good, that we may share in his holiness. No discipline seems pleasant at the time, but painful. Later on, however, it produces a harvest of righteousness and peace for those who have been trained by it. Therefore, strengthen your feeble arms and weak knees. Make level paths for your feet, so that the lame may not be disabled, but rather healed. Make every effort to live in peace with all men and to be holy; *without holiness no one will see the Lord.*

The final password is *holiness*. What is holiness? I know what you're thinking. There's no way, I don't feel like I could ever be holy—holiness is a complicated concept and the word can mean different things. I agree, just look at this short paragraph I copied from Holman Bible Dictionary (this was just a small section!):

HOLY A characteristic unique to God's nature, which becomes the goal for human moral character. The idea of "holy" is important for an understanding of God, of worship, and of the people of God in the Bible. Holy has four distinct meanings. First is "to be set apart." This applies to places where God is present, like the Temple and the tabernacle, and to things and persons related to those holy places or to God Himself. Next, it means to be "perfect, transcendent, or spiritually pure, evoking adoration and reverence." This applies primarily to God, but secondarily to saints or godly people. Next, it means something or someone who evokes "veneration or awe, being frightening beyond belief." This is clearly the application to God and is the primary meaning of "holy." It is continued in the last definition, "filled with superhuman and potential fatal power." This speaks of God, but also of places or things or persons which have been set apart by God's presence. A saint is a holy person. To be sanctified is to be made holy.

I found the above definition to be a little confusing. I think holiness is either *perfect or practical*. God, our Creator, is *perfect* holiness. He is "set apart." He is absolute righteousness, spiritually pure. He alone evokes adoration, reverence, awe, and is frightening beyond belief. Our God is a consuming fire!

Hebrews 12:28-29 (NIV)
Therefore, since we are receiving a kingdom that cannot be shaken, let us be thankful, and so worship God acceptably with reverence and awe, for our "God is a consuming fire."

Practical holiness is what we are to be about. The Creator is *perfectly* holy; we, the creation, are to be *practically* holy. What's the difference? Let's face it, we are not God (nor are we little gods) and *perfect* holiness is unattainable. Remember, however, that with the "instantaneous transformation" we received as a *gift*, the righteousness of Christ. This allows God to see Jesus' *perfect* holiness when He looks at us. Only this *perfect* holiness will allow us access into heaven and into God's presence. So that's it? What about *practical* holiness? I think this is more of an *attitude* than anything else. We should humbly admit that we fall short but God does find pleasure in the person whose attitude is focused on pleasing Him. Evangelist Ron Hutchcraft says it like this:

God gives His best to those who are passionate about being pure...who are aggressively cleaning out their remaining dirty closets, not content with just status quo holiness. The Lord rewards you because you always do what you do by the book—His Book, the Bible—from how you handle the money, to how you handle problems, to how you handle people. He's looking for stubborn integrity...zero tolerance for sin and compromise in your life...a desire to be, as one great preacher said, "as holy a person as a redeemed sinner can be."

We can't earn our relationship with God - heaven is based on us trusting completely in the work **Jesus** did on the cross. But God's **rewards**- not only in heaven, but here on earth - are based on how we live. And He's got His eye on you. He has some wonderful life-bonuses He wants to give you. But He's a holy God. He can only reward **holiness**.

Make that the goal that drives you—to be totally His man or His woman. Because if God is impressed with you, you are unlocking heaven's blessing gate - which is bolted on our side, not His. He's looking for someone after His own holy heart. Or, in God's own words, *"The eyes of the Lord range throughout the earth to strengthen those whose hearts are fully committed to Him" (II Chronicles 16:9).*

What happens if you fail? That's all right because that's where grace fits into the picture. Grace makes up for all the shortcomings. Grace says, "You're O.K., get up my child and try again." Grace is the link, the connection, between the *perfect* and the *practical*.

Finally, all three words are typed in and the door opens into the workshop of the Almighty. You have demonstrated a humble attitude and have hungered for Him. You are now in his presence and when He sees you He sees only His son Jesus Christ—*perfect holiness*. How should we enter into this most sacred place?

Psalm 100:3-5 (NIV)
Know that the LORD is God. It is he who made us, and we are his; we are his people, the sheep of his pasture. Enter his gates *with thanksgiving* and his courts *with praise*; give thanks to him and praise his name. For the LORD is good and his love endures forever; his faithfulness continues through all generations.

We enter with thanksgiving and praise! Thank Him for providing you with salvation and for all that He has blessed us with.

James 1:16-17(NIV)
Don't be deceived, my dear brothers. *Every good and perfect gift is from above*, coming down from the Father of the heavenly lights, who does not change like shifting shadows.

God will then ask you – "What do you seek my child?" Your heart is pounding; what do you say? Remember that Jesus gave us an answer.

Matthew 6:33 (NIV)
But seek first his kingdom and his righteousness, and all these things will be given to you as well.

Matthew 7:7-8 (NIV)
"Ask and it will be given to you; seek and you will find; knock and the door will be opened to you. For

everyone who asks receives; he who seeks finds; and to him who knocks, the door will be opened.

What is the Kingdom of God? Simply put, I believe it is the ultimate fulfillment of God's will in Heaven and on earth. We need to realize that He has a plan, purpose, and destiny, for our lives. When we enter into His "workshop" our ultimate goal should be to search out, and chase after, *God's* will for our life. It is a complete surrendering of your life to Him.

"God, I have been created by you to bring you glory—please show me your plan, purpose, and destiny for my life. I am here to serve you—what will you have me do?"

Remember, this is a place to start in the workshop. Where do we go from here? Jesus made a fascinating promise in the following verse.

Matthew 17:20 (NIV)
> He replied, "Because you have so little faith. I tell you the truth, if you have faith as small as a mustard seed, you can say to this mountain, 'Move from here to there' and it will move. Nothing will be impossible for you."

I had always struggled with this verse because I felt that anyone who had demonstrated enough faith to believe in Jesus Christ and experience the "instantaneous transformation" *surely* had faith the size of a tiny little mustard seed. I had many times attempted to move mountains and never achieved success. I couldn't seem to move even a little rock, let alone a mountain! But then, a couple of chapter's later, Jesus spoke a parable that I think helps to answer the dilemma.

Matthew 13:31-32 (NIV)
> He told them another parable: "The kingdom of

heaven is like a mustard seed, which a man took and planted in his field. Though it is the smallest of all your seeds, yet when it grows, it is the largest of garden plants and becomes a tree, so that the birds of the air come and perch in its branches."

It finally made sense! Our faith starts as a tiny mustard seed, but it has to grow *as only God can cause it to grow*. It is a slow, steady process. The seed sprouts and begins to grow, it requires nourishment, sunlight, water, and ultimately, if growing conditions remain favorable, it will develop into a large tree with "branches for the birds of the air to come and perch in." God causes our faith to grow. We can't move mountains when we are just a tiny mustard seed, but as we grow in faith we'll begin to see miracles, signs, and wonders. God will reveal Himself in powerful ways. Eventually, if we continue growing, we will be able to move mountains. Jesus promised that we would, and could, do even greater miracles then He did.

John 14:9-14 (NIV)
Jesus answered: "Don't you know me, Philip, even after I have been among you such a long time? Anyone who has seen me has seen the Father. How can you say, 'Show us the Father'? Don't you believe that I am in the Father, and that the Father is in me? The words I say to you are not just my own. Rather, it is the Father, living in me, who is doing his work. Believe me when I say that I am in the Father and the Father is in me; or at least believe on the evidence of the miracles themselves. *I tell you the truth, anyone who has faith in me will do what I have been doing. He will do even greater things than these, because I am going to the Father.* And I will do whatever you ask in my

name, so that the Son may bring glory to the Father. You may ask me for anything in my name, and I will do it.

In summary, we've discovered that we all, as Christians, have the Spirit of the living God within us. Only this Spirit can bring about the changes we long for in our lives. Only this Spirit can show us what the will of God is. The Kingdom of God is within every Christian. We open the door to God's "workshop" via *humility, hunger, holiness*, and enter in with *thanksgiving and praise*. We are then in a position to allow God to change us *from the inside out*—to literally change our hearts. Remember this is a slow, steady process. There is no shortcut, no quick fix. Very simply— God cannot conform us to the likeness of His Son unless we give Him the time, and opportunity, to bring about the changes. This brings us to the concept talked about by Richard J. Foster in his book "Celebration of Discipline— the Path to Spiritual Growth." He simply calls it "the path of disciplined grace—It is 'grace' because it is free; it is 'discipline' because there is something for us to do." This is the subject of the next chapter—a discussion of what I see as the key *spiritual disciplines* practiced by our master, Jesus Christ, when He walked on this earth ~2000 years ago. We will come to understand, and apply, the disciplines as part of what goes on *inside* God's "workshop." Let's discover these hidden treasures!

— Chapter 5 —

I HATE THAT WORD "DISCIPLINE"

Our society, unfortunately, has come to a place where *instant gratification* is the rule. It's been called the "McDonald's mentality"—I want it now, not later. Don't make me wait. How much longer is it going to be? I believe that this mindset has become a curse upon our society. It has carried over into our lives and it has affected many areas—especially the spiritual ones. It is been said that "patience is a virtue"—a noble quality. I think God agrees. It is one of the "fruits" of the Holy Spirit.

> **Galatians 5:22-23 (NIV)**
> But the fruit of the Spirit is love, joy, peace, *patience*, kindness, goodness, faithfulness, gentleness and self-control. Against such things there is no law.

Look at what the Apostle Paul said about the "patience" of Jesus:

1 Timothy 1:15-16 (NIV)
Here is a trustworthy saying that deserves full acceptance: Christ Jesus came into the world to save sinners—of whom I am the worst. But for that very reason I was shown mercy so that in me, the worst of sinners, Christ Jesus might display his *unlimited patience* as an example for those who would believe on him and receive eternal life.

He is *so patient* that often it's misinterpreted by people as "slowness."

2 Peter 3:8-9 (NIV)
But do not forget this one thing, dear friends: With the Lord a day is like a thousand years, and a thousand years are like a day. The Lord is not slow in keeping his promise, as some understand slowness. He is patient with you, not wanting anyone to perish, but everyone to come to repentance.

What else does God say about "patience?" He asks that we be patient not only with Him...

Psalm 37:7 (NIV)
Be still before the LORD and wait patiently for him; do not fret when men succeed in their ways, when they carry out their wicked schemes.

Psalm 40:1 (NIV)
I waited patiently for the LORD; he turned to me and heard my cry.

...but that we also be patient with others:

I Hate That Word "Discipline"

1 Thessalonians 5:14 (NIV)
And we urge you, brothers, warn those who are idle, encourage the timid, help the weak, be patient with everyone.

I think "patience" has become a practical problem for us because it correlates with *time*. We all have been given 24 hours a day, but in our "rat-race" society it never seems to be enough. The first place we surrender time is in the spiritual area (the "spiritual disciplines"). We cut short our time with God. Why? I believe it ultimately has to do with feelings of self-sufficiency. We think we can do it on our own. This, as we've already discussed, is pride. The next area we slate for "budget cuts" relates to our own physical health. Exercise, a healthy diet, and rest (the "physical disciplines") very often get pushed to the "back burner"—or no "burner" at all! In summary, it simply boils down to *time*—God has given all of us the same amount to use everyday. Once used, it can never be retrieved again. Our goal should be to get the very most out of everyday—to make the best of the time that we've been given. I believe that if we give God a small *investment* of time *everyday*, and revive the "spiritual and physical disciplines", we will see our productivity and energy levels soar! We begin to think God's thoughts—to have the "mind of Christ"—and the dividends on our investment will be substantial.

Now we begin our discussion of **discipline**. You just squirmed, didn't you? Almost everyone cringes when they even hear the word. Why does it elicit such a response? Quite simply, discipline usually correlates with pain—we all love pain, don't we?!

Hebrews 12:7-11 (NIV)
Endure hardship as discipline; God is treating you as sons. For what son is not disciplined by his

father? If you are not disciplined (and everyone undergoes discipline), then you are illegitimate children and not true sons. Moreover, we have all had human fathers who disciplined us and we respected them for it. How much more should we submit to the Father of our spirits and live! Our fathers disciplined us for a little while as they thought best; but God disciplines us for our good, that we may share in his holiness. No discipline seems pleasant at the time, but painful. Later on, however, it produces a harvest of righteousness and peace for those who have been trained by it.

Discipline can be imposed by any authority figure (God, parents, boss, etc.) as discussed in the above verse, or *self-imposed*. Our discussion will, for now, be limited to the latter. What we choose to do to ourselves. In this passage Paul talks about *self-imposed discipline*:

1 Corinthians 9:24-27 (NIV)
Do you not know that in a race all the runners run, but only one gets the prize? Run in such a way as to get the prize. Everyone who competes in the games goes into *strict training*. They do it to get a crown that will not last; but we do it to get a crown that will last forever. Therefore I do not run like a man running aimlessly; I do not fight like a man beating the air. No, I beat my body and make it my slave so that after I have preached to others, I myself will not be disqualified for the prize.

It's like any athlete training for their sport. The greatest athletes have undeniably been the most disciplined behind the scenes. They have been patient and have "put in their time." "No pain, no gain" is their motto. This is the essence of self-imposed discipline. Please note, however, that it is self-imposed—no one else can do it to you, or for you. It is *patient, sometimes painful, discipline*. It is the method most often used by God to bring about lasting change in a person's life. Can God bring about miraculous, instantaneous change? Yes, He can, and He still does! You have to admit, however, this is not the primary method for bringing about change. Christians will experience the changes they're longing for only when they understand how God uses patient, sometimes painful, discipline—*seasoned with grace*—to bring them about. We talked a lot about seeds in chapter two and it would be worthwhile to briefly review this beautiful illustration.

A seed will not grow until it's first placed into the right soil (environment). If conditions remain favorable (proper sunlight, water, and temperature) slow changes begin to occur—the seed sprouts and begins to grow *as God causes it to grow*. Eventually, it will grow into a fine plant that, hopefully, bears much fruit. This requires patience and takes time. Our responsibility is to make sure we get into the right environment (God's workshop) so that God can do a work in our lives—sometimes God's "pruning" (God-imposed discipline) is painful, but this is where we can also help to bring about change by using the process of *patient, sometimes painful, discipline—seasoned with grace*. This will act as "fertilizer" to supercharge our growth. Always remember, however, God brings about the real changes.

What are the "spiritual and physical disciplines" we've been talking about? How can we use them properly and not legalistically (as rules and laws)? We will start with the most important—the "spiritual disciplines." The Apostle Paul agreed that the "physical disciplines" were "of value", but the "spiritual disciplines" should be our priority.

1 Timothy 4:8 (NIV)
For physical training is of some value, but godliness has value for all things, holding promise for both the present life and the life to come.

The early church practiced them routinely, but, as time passed, the disciplines went from being beneficial and practical to destructive and legalistic. Legalism kills interest faster than anything else I know. I think we should look at Jesus as our example and keep it simple. Jesus practiced the "spiritual disciplines" either alone (solitude) or in groups (small or large).

Jesus would commonly retreat to a place to be alone.

Luke 5:16 (NIV)
But Jesus often withdrew to lonely places and prayed.

This is the foremost spiritual discipline: **solitude.** I believe it was Jesus' secret weapon. It is the platform from which many of the other disciplines spring. We have already discussed this process—getting into "God's workshop." *You have to get alone with God!* We saw that it required humility, hunger, and holiness. Now what? The next discipline is **prayer.** Prayer! What is prayer? Simply put, it's communication with God. You talk with Him just as you would your best friend. I know that sounds like an oversimplification, however, the problem with trying to come up with a definition for prayer is similar to what we experienced with the concept of "holy." There are many facets (sub-disciplines) to prayer—I will try to give you a simplified explanation.

The Apostle Paul talked about praying two ways: with your mind and with your Spirit (the Holy Spirit living in every true believer). Read this short passage.

1 Corinthians 14:13-17 (NIV)
For this reason anyone who speaks in a tongue should pray that he may interpret what he says. For if I pray in a tongue, my spirit prays, but my mind is unfruitful. So what shall I do? I will pray with my spirit, but I will also pray with my mind; I will sing with my spirit, but I will also sing with my mind. If you are praising God with your spirit, how can one who finds himself among those who do not understand say "Amen" to your thanksgiving, since he does not know what you are saying? You may be giving thanks well enough, but the other man is not edified.

Paul is specifically talking about the "gift" of speaking in tongues. I know what you're thinking—this has been a topic that has caused much controversy and even divisions in the church. In short, it is the language of the Holy Spirit. Those of you who have experienced it know what I'm talking about; for the rest of you, this is just a point of clarification so that the above passage makes more sense. The only point I wanted to make is that we can pray with our mind *and* with our Spirit (i.e. the Holy Spirit). Which is better? Obviously, when you are praying in the Spirit, you are *perfectly* praying the will of God. The Holy Spirit is a person (part of the Trinity). Confused? Read this verse.

Romans 8:26-27 (NIV)
In the same way, the Spirit helps us in our weakness. We do not know what we ought to pray for, but the Spirit himself intercedes for us with groans that words cannot express. And he who searches our hearts knows the mind of the Spirit, because the Spirit intercedes for the saints in accordance with God's will.

In reality, we pray primarily with our mind. This is not a bad thing, but, as you can imagine, there will be times when we may pray for something that God knows may harm us or not be beneficial to His Kingdom (consistent with His will and purpose). What's the ultimate goal? That we eventually conform our mind to His mind—our will to His will. On this earth we will always be praying with both our mind and Spirit. As long as we live in this physical body this is how it is done. When we pray what we know is God's will, then what Jesus promised in these verses finally makes sense.

John 14:13-14 (NIV)
And I will do whatever you ask in my name, so that the Son may bring glory to the Father. You may ask me for anything in my name, and I will do it.

John 16:23b-24 (NIV)
I tell you the truth, my Father will give you whatever you ask in my name. Until now you have not asked for anything in my name. Ask and you will receive, and your joy will be complete.

Prayer is a *process*—it's part of the "gradual transformation" that we have discussed before. It's how we experience the transformation (renewing) of our minds.

Romans 12:1-2 (NIV)
Therefore, I urge you, brothers, in view of God's mercy, to offer your bodies as living sacrifices, holy and pleasing to God—this is your spiritual act of worship. Do not conform any longer to the pattern of this world, but *be transformed by the renewing of your mind.* Then you will be able to test and approve what God's will is—his good, pleasing and perfect will.

The essence of the *process of prayer* is one of trust. Do you trust that the God who spoke the universe into existence, who "knows the very number of hairs on your head", can lead you to the perfect peace and joy that He promises? Yes, a thousand times, yes!

Obviously, praying in the Spirit is a "God-thing." We really have no control over this. We do, however, have control over how we pray with our mind. Luckily, Jesus gave us a perfect model for how we should pray with our mind. I like to call this *"practical prayer."*

Matthew 6:9-13 (NIV)
"This, then, is how you should pray: "'Our Father in heaven, hallowed be your name, your kingdom come, your will be done on earth as it is in heaven. Give us today our daily bread. Forgive us our debts, as we also have forgiven our debtors. And lead us not into temptation, but deliver us from the evil one.'

What can we glean from Jesus' model of prayer?

- God desires that it be *intimate* and *personal.*
- God is worthy of *worship, praise,* and *thanksgiving* and is all sufficient—able to meet *all* our needs.
- God desires *submission* and *surrender* to Him and His will for our life.
- Present your *requests* to God—your daily needs.
- *Confession* of our sin and power to *forgive others* who have sinned against us.
- *Empowered* by the Holy Spirit to be pure and holy—to be kept from temptation and delivered from Satan.

Doesn't the Bible say that we are to "pray continually?"

1 Thessalonians 5:16-18 (NIV)
Be joyful always; *pray continually*; give thanks in all circumstances, for this is God's will for you in Christ Jesus.

How can we pray *continually*? Remember, prayer is a process—we are being gradually transformed into the "likeness of Christ." Practically speaking, however, we still have to *discipline* ourselves to give God the time and opportunity to make the transformation. The process starts with "practical prayer", following the model Jesus gave to us; it then begins to build upon itself. Simply put, what God desires is some of our time. If we can discipline ourselves to enter His workshop, and communicate with Him by prayer (following His model), He will conform us *gradually* to the likeness of His Son, Jesus Christ. This will allow the Holy Spirit of Jesus Christ, living inside you, to make the transformations you so desire. You'll begin to have perfect peace, joy, happiness, and all the other "fruits of the Spirit." You'll begin to have the "abundant life" that Jesus talked about. People will begin to see the changes in your life and God will use you in ways you never dreamed were possible. How much time? I cannot answer this any other way than to say "some" time—*just start and see what God does*. Challenge Him to change you and soon you'll see that you can't wait to spend time in His "workshop" where you can be in His presence. True Christianity is not a religion, but a relationship—a relationship with God, the Father, through his Son, Jesus Christ. If you will cultivate this relationship with time, effort, and commitment, you'll reap great benefits and rewards. This same principle applies to marriage and any other relationship as well.

I Hate That Word "Discipline"

So, in our time of solitude we can pray, but sometimes we need to practice the discipline of **silence** before God. Listen for His voice—He will speak to you through the Holy Spirit. This is what people mean when they say that God told them to do something or that God talked to them. They were practicing the discipline of silence and listening for the voice of God. Is it an audible voice? Usually not. The point is that we will have difficulty hearing God if we never shut up. That's all I have to say about that!

Psalm 46:10 (NIV)
"Be still, and know that I am God; I will be exalted among the nations, I will be exalted in the earth."

Another key discipline commonly slighted by Christians is **reading, studying, and meditating upon the Word of God**. In our discussion of the Lord's Prayer above, we talked about submission and surrender to the will of God. This was the part of the prayer where Jesus said "your kingdom come, your will be done on earth as it is in heaven." Obviously, the Holy Spirit can (and does) make us aware of God's will, but many fail to understand that the Bible contains the very Word of God and is in perfect harmony with the will of God. It contains God's answers to virtually all of life's problems. What did the Apostle Paul say about scripture (the Bible)?

2 Timothy 3:16-17 (NIV)
All Scripture is God-breathed and is useful for teaching, rebuking, correcting and training in righteousness, so that the man of God may be thoroughly equipped for every good work.

Wow! God-breathed. This is why you see Christians hauling their Bibles everywhere. It is because they recognize the power and authority of the Word of God. The Bible has numerous prophetic passages (some already fulfilled, many yet to be fulfilled), which speak to its truth and relevance. Where did the prophets get their material?

2 Peter 1:20-21 (NIV)
Above all, you must understand that no prophecy of Scripture came about by the prophet's own interpretation. For prophecy never had its origin in the will of man, but men spoke from God as they were carried along by the Holy Spirit.

What other claims are made about scripture?

Hebrews 4:12-13 (NIV)
For the word of God is living and active. Sharper than any double-edged sword, it penetrates even to dividing soul and spirit, joints and marrow; it judges the thoughts and attitudes of the heart. Nothing in all creation is hidden from God's sight. Everything is uncovered and laid bare before the eyes of him to whom we must give account.

If the Word of God is "living and active" then it must be a person—right? Read this powerful passage from John's gospel:

John 1:1-14 (NIV)
In the beginning was the Word, and the Word was with God, and the Word was God. He was with God in the beginning. Through him all things were made; without him nothing was made that has been made. In him was life, and that life was the light of men. The light shines in the darkness, but the darkness has not understood it. There came a man who

was sent from God; his name was John. He came as a witness to testify concerning that light, so that through him all men might believe. He himself was not the light; he came only as a witness to the light. The true light that gives light to every man was coming into the world._ He was in the world, and though the world was made through him, the world did not recognize him. He came to that which was his own, but his own did not receive him. Yet to all who received him, to those who believed in his name, he gave the right to become children of God—children born not of natural descent, nor of human decision or a husband's will, but born of God. ***The Word became flesh and made his dwelling among us.*** We have seen his glory, the glory of the One and Only, who came from the Father, full of grace and truth.

Jesus Christ is the Word! Do you remember what Jesus said about Himself?

John 14:6 (NIV)
Jesus answered, "I am the way and the truth and the life. No one comes to the Father except through me.

We can only conclude then that the Word is truth and life. It's all *intimately* connected together. When we are "born again" and receive God's Holy Spirit we get the Word literally into our very being—into our hearts and mind.

Hebrews 10:15-17 (NIV)
The Holy Spirit also testifies to us about this. First he says: "This is the covenant I will make with them after that time, says the Lord. *I will put my*

> *laws in their hearts, and I will write them on their minds.*" Then he adds: "Their sins and lawless acts I will remember no more."

How do reading, studying, and meditating on the Word of God correlate with prayer? We talked about praying with both our mind and Spirit—recognizing that praying "in the Spirit" was a *God-thing* and that the discipline of prayer involved practical application (practical prayer) using Jesus' model to guide us. We do, indeed, have the very law of God written on our hearts and in our minds, however, this also is a "God-thing." I don't know about you, but when I became a "born-again" Christian I didn't automatically begin practicing every law God had written upon my heart. Trust me—God has done this for every believer, but it is like prayer. It's a *process* as well and it needs to develop and grow. How do we achieve this? We begin to practice the discipline of reading, studying, and meditating on the Word of God—this will literally feed your Spirit. This, along with prayer, is a perfect discipline to practice during your time of solitude.

Proverbs 7:1-3 (NIV)
> My son, keep my words and store up my commands within you. Keep my commands and you will live; guard my teachings as the apple of your eye. Bind them on your fingers; write them on the tablet of your heart.

I know many of you are thinking, "The Bible is too hard to understand." "There are just too many different interpretations"—wrong answer. There is just one interpretation and that is God's interpretation. The secret is to let the Holy Spirit do the interpreting for you.

I Hate That Word "Discipline"

1 Corinthians 2:10b-16 (NIV)
The Spirit searches all things, even the deep things of God. For who among men knows the thoughts of a man except the man's spirit within him? *In the same way no one knows the thoughts of God except the Spirit of God.* We have not received the spirit of the world but the Spirit who is from God, that we may understand what God has freely given us. This is what we speak, not in words taught us by human wisdom but in words taught by the Spirit, expressing spiritual truths in spiritual words. The man without the Spirit does not accept the things that come from the Spirit of God, for they are foolishness to him, and he cannot understand them, because they are spiritually discerned. The spiritual man makes judgments about all things, but he himself is not subject to any man's judgment: "For who has known the mind of the Lord that he may instruct him? But we have the mind of Christ.

I had a neat experience when I became a Christian. I had read the Bible before I had experienced the "instantaneous transformation" and it made little sense. Honestly, I found it to be rather boring. Afterwards, it was like a veil had been lifted from my eyes—all of a sudden it began to make sense! What had happened? I had been given *new eyes*—the eyes of the Holy Spirit. I found it exhilarating and couldn't get enough. It doesn't take Satan long to begin his attack in this area. He understands how powerful God's word is. Remember what Jesus did in the wilderness when He was tempted? That's right. He quoted scripture.

Matthew 4:4 (NIV)
Jesus answered, "It is written: 'Man does not live on bread alone, but on every word that comes from the mouth of God.'"

Satan will do whatever he can to keep you from this discipline.

All of the disciplines talked about so far have been discussed within the context of the discipline of solitude. Remember, however, that Jesus spent a lot of time in groups (small and large)—both with His disciples and with large crowds. He obviously thought that being with other people was important. This is called **fellowship** with other believers—and is also a "spiritual discipline."

Hebrews 10:25 (NIV)
Let us not give up meeting together, as some are in the habit of doing, but let us encourage one another—and all the more as you see the Day approaching.

For the outgoing, social type, it's a somewhat less trying discipline, however, for those of us who are introverts—whew, this one can be tough! Note that most of the disciplines already discussed can also be done within the context of fellowship.

How does God use other Christians to help us mature in our Christian walk? *He uses other Christians to encourage and teach us.* We are all aware of how God used the prophets in the Old Testament as his voice. We, however, have the privilege of having other Christians (who have God's Spirit within them) to help us. Remember, we are all at different stages in our "walk."

Proverbs 27:17 (NIV)
As iron sharpens iron, so one man sharpens another.

Colossians 1:28 (NIV)
We proclaim him, *admonishing and teaching everyone with all wisdom*, so that we may present everyone perfect in Christ.

Colossians 3:16 (NIV)
Let the word of Christ dwell in you richly as you *teach and admonish one another with all wisdom*, and as you sing psalms, hymns and spiritual songs with gratitude in your hearts to God.

What are some other benefits of fellowship? *God says there is power in numbers.* Praying with other Christians unleashes the power of God.

Matthew 18:19-20 (NIV)
"Again, I tell you that if two of you on earth agree about anything you ask for, it will be done for you by my Father in heaven. For where two or three come together in my name, there am I with them."

God's ultimate plan is to blend us together to be *one body*—that there be a unification of our different gifts and talents. Why? A unified body will ultimately be the most effective, powerful force to further God's kingdom. Again, there is power in numbers.

1 Corinthians 12:12-31 (NIV)
The body is a unit, though it is made up of many parts; and though all its parts are many, they form one body. So it is with Christ. For we were all baptized by one Spirit into one body—whether Jews

or Greeks, slave or free—and we were all given the one Spirit to drink. Now the body is not made up of one part but of many. If the foot should say, "Because I am not a hand, I do not belong to the body," it would not for that reason cease to be part of the body. And if the ear should say, "Because I am not an eye, I do not belong to the body," it would not for that reason cease to be part of the body. If the whole body were an eye, where would the sense of hearing be? If the whole body were an ear, where would the sense of smell be? But in fact God has arranged the parts in the body, every one of them, just as he wanted them to be. If they were all one part, where would the body be? As it is, there are many parts, but one body. The eye cannot say to the hand, "I don't need you!" And the head cannot say to the feet, "I don't need you!" On the contrary, those parts of the body that seem to be weaker are indispensable, and the parts that we think are less honorable we treat with special honor. And the parts that are unpresentable are treated with special modesty, while our presentable parts need no special treatment. But God has combined the members of the body and has given greater honor to the parts that lacked it, so that there should be no division in the body, but that its parts should have equal concern for each other. If one part suffers, every part suffers with it; if one part is honored, every part rejoices with it. Now you are the body of Christ, and each one of you is a part of it. And in the church God has appointed first of all apostles, second prophets, third teachers, then workers of miracles, also those having gifts of healing, those able to help others, those with gifts of administration, and those speaking in different kinds of tongues. Are all apostles? Are all prophets? Are all teachers? Do all work miracles? Do all have gifts of healing? Do all speak in tongues? Do all interpret? But eagerly desire the greater gifts.

Lastly, we have been instructed to be *accountable* to other "believers"—don't be afraid to have a close Christian friend who will not be afraid to ask you "the tough questions." Confide in this individual and ask them to pray specifically for your special need(s).

James 5:16 (NIV)
Therefore confess your sins to each other and pray for each other so that you may be healed. The prayer of a righteous man is powerful and effective.

Practically speaking, we can practice the discipline of fellowship (and all it's sub-disciplines) by finding a "good" church. What do I mean by "good?" A church that believes that the Bible is literally God's word to mankind and that Jesus Christ is the only way to God. Ask God to help you find a "good" church!

James 1:5 (NIV)
If any of you lacks wisdom, he should ask God, who gives generously to all without finding fault, and it will be given to him.

Now that we've completed our discussion of the "spiritual disciplines" it's time to switch our focus—on to the "physical disciplines!"
Remember, we started our discussion of the "spiritual disciplines" by emphasizing that spiritual > physical.

1 Timothy 4:8 (NIV)
For physical training is of some value, but godliness has value for all things, holding promise for both the present life and the life to come.

I want you to understand, however, that God also desires discipline when it comes to taking care of our physical body. We talked in earlier chapters about the fact that we're triune beings: body, soul, and Spirit. Our soul and Spirit are nurtured by practicing the "spiritual disciplines." We can nurture (and nourish) our body by practicing the "physical disciplines." God says that our body is "a temple of the Holy Spirit."

1 Corinthians 6:19-20 (NIV)
Do you not know that your body is a *temple of the Holy Spirit*, who is in you, whom you have received from God? You are not your own; you were bought at a price. Therefore honor God with your body.

God wants us to "purify" from our lives everything that would contaminate our body or Spirit.

2 Corinthians 7:1 (NIV)
Since we have these promises, dear friends, let us *purify ourselves from everything that contaminates body and spirit*, perfecting holiness out of reverence for God.

I firmly believe that if we institute the "physical disciplines" simultaneously with the "spiritual disciplines" the changes will be profound. What are the *three* key physical disciplines?

I Hate That Word "Discipline"

1. A well-balanced, **healthy diet**
2. Regular aerobic **exercise**
3. Adequate **rest** (good sleep habits) and relaxation

Let's now discuss each in a little more detail.

What is a healthy diet? What a topic! Everyone has an idea, an exclusive diet. Countless books have been written on this subject. Medical knowledge is growing rapidly in the area of nutrition and I believe we are beginning to understand that our diets have a profound impact on our well-being—more than we ever imagined. We're beginning to understand the wisdom in the statement, "You are what you eat." Many of the illnesses more common in America have to do with improper dietary habits and obesity: hypertension, diabetes, depression, and chronic fatigue to name a few. This book is not intended to be the answer for what is the "correct" diet. Suffice it to say, I believe that simplicity is the key. We need to get back to foods in their natural, wholesome state—fruits and vegetables, whole-grain breads and cereals, fish and poultry, and *lots* of water (filtered is best). You can add in a multi-vitamin/mineral product if you wish. Avoid highly processed foods, artificial *anything* (especially sweeteners), saturated fats, and too much caffeine. Jesus ate fruit, nuts, whole-grain breads, and fish. His diet was very natural—high in fiber, low in fat. I think most people have a good grasp on what constitutes a "healthy" diet. We need, however, not just to *know*, but also to *do*!

A related problem is our tendency to *overeat*. I mentioned it earlier when we were talking about addictions. I believe that it is, first and foremost, a spiritual problem. Most of the successful "weight-loss" programs deal with it on a spiritual level. Most will agree that eating is pleasurable—God designed it that way! However, after that "big" meal you feel sluggish and slow, and then you say, "I wish I hadn't eaten so much." We have become extremists when it comes to "eating out." Why? Convenience and entertainment! God has blessed this great nation with a marvelous abundance, but, once again, we've "pushed the envelope" and have turned the blessing into a curse. Most people in the world do not have enough to eat and go to bed hungry. Don't forget to thank God for what He's given us!

Losing weight *mathematically* is really very simple:

$$\text{Calories in} < \text{Calories out}$$

It takes 3000 calories (kcal) to equal 1 pound of fat. How many calories do we need in a day? It ultimately depends upon our activity level, but everyone has what's known as a "basal metabolic rate" (BMR). This is the number of calories you need to carry on all the "behind the scenes" activity in your physical body—to keep your heart beating, breathing, etc. It's the number of calories that you need just to exist as a living being.

Here's a quick formula to estimate:

Women: 661 + (4.38 x weight in pounds) + (4.33 x height in inches) - (4.7 x age) = BMR

Men: 67 + (6.24 x weight in pounds) + (12.7 x height in inches) - (6.9 x age) = BMR

To estimate the total number of calories your body needs per day, multiply your BMR by the appropriate number below.

- 0.9 if you are inactive and have crash dieted frequently during the past two years.
- 1.2 if you are inactive
- 1.3 if you are moderately active (exercise 3 days per week or equivalent)
- 1.7 if you are very active
- 1.9 if you are extremely active.

Most BMR's for adults range between 1500—2500 calories. Let's say that your BMR is roughly 2000 calories/day daily and you decrease your caloric intake by only 200 calories per day: your total now is 1800 calories. We said 3000 calories equals 1 pound of fat, therefore, in 15 days you would lose 1 pound of fat, about 24 pounds in a year! Remember, however, it works in reverse the same way! If calories in = calories out then your weight will remain stable.

Where does exercise fit into this picture? Not only does it "burn" calories, it will actually increase your overall BMR—it "revs up the engine" so to speak. Exercise is another "physical discipline" that will pay big dividends for a small investment. Again, numerous books exist to try and tell you how to get physically fit. It can make your head spin! As a general rule, however, any activity that increases your heart rate to 60-80% of your "target" heart rate, for 20 to 30 minutes, 3 to 5 times per week, is all you need. It can be brisk walking, jogging, bicycling, jumping rope, climbing hills, or whatever you want. Jesus walked miles every day and I imagine He was in great shape.

How can you calculate your target heart rate? The simplest way to calculate your Target Heart Rate is to subtract your age from 220. This number is the maximum times your heart can beat (effectively) in one minute. **If you are just beginning**, your target heart rate should be between 60 to 75% of your maximum heart rate but after six months you can safely exercise up to 85%.

Lastly, we discuss the discipline of rest and relaxation. It would seem, on the surface, that we Americans have this one down. I'm not so sure. Everyone takes casually what Benjamin Franklin said "Early to bed, early to rise, makes a man healthy wealthy and wise", however, the older I get the more wisdom I see in this statement. One of the most difficult things I had to do, working as a physician in the Emergency Room, was to bounce shifts around—days to nights, nights to days—never any routine. This made it very challenging to consistently institute *any discipline*, whether it is "spiritual" or "physical." Jesus knew the importance of regular rest, not only adequate time for sleep, but time for relaxation. He commonly combined His relaxation with fellowship (as can we)—not only with other believers, but also sometimes with "sinners and tax-collectors."

> **Matthew 9:10-13 (NIV)**
> While Jesus was having dinner at Matthew's house, many tax collectors and "sinners" came and ate with him and his disciples. When the Pharisees saw this, they asked his disciples, "Why does your teacher eat with tax collectors and 'sinners'? On hearing this, Jesus said, "It is not the healthy who need a doctor, but the sick. But go and learn what this means: 'I desire mercy, not sacrifice.' For I have not come to call the righteous, but sinners."

How important is rest? God gave the Israelites the Sabbath—a day of rest. He even made it one of the Ten Commandments!

> **Exodus 20:8-11 (NIV)**
> "Remember the Sabbath day by keeping it holy. Six days you shall labor and do all your work, but the seventh day is a Sabbath to the Lord your God. On it you shall not do any work, neither you, nor your son or daughter, nor your manservant or maidservant, nor your animals, nor the alien within your gates. For in six days the Lord made the heavens and the earth, the sea, and all that is in them, but he rested on the seventh day. Therefore the Lord blessed the Sabbath day and made it holy.

I Hate That Word "Discipline"

I didn't want to digress too much on the physical disciplines, but I feel that very few Christians apply *both* the "spiritual" and "physical" disciplines to their lives. Remember, our bodies are a "temple" of the Holy Spirit (1 Corinthians 6:19-20) (NIV).

I want to finish my "discourse on the disciplines" with a challenging, thought provoking discussion of what I believe is the *forgotten discipline*: **fasting**. I know what your thinking—"that isn't healthy, I'll get sick." I realize there are some people with certain health problems who have to be very careful with this one—please use a little common sense. However, all of the "saints" in God's Hall of Fame *fasted*—Moses, Daniel, all of the prophets, the Disciples, and Paul, to name a few! It was a very common practice in the early Church—most often done in conjunction with prayer. Most importantly, Jesus did it! I figure that if it's all right for Jesus then it must be all right for us.

Matthew 4:1-2 (NIV)
> Then Jesus was led by the Spirit into the desert to be tempted by the devil. After fasting forty days and forty nights, he was hungry.

It's my opinion that *fasting* is the one discipline that ties the "spiritual" and "physical" disciplines together. If you want to *turbo charge* any of the disciplines (especially the "spiritual") then consider a *fast*. There was a demon that the Disciples couldn't cast out—look at what Jesus taught them.

Mark 9:17-29 (NIV)
> A man in the crowd answered, "Teacher, I brought you my son, who is possessed by a spirit that has robbed him of speech. Whenever it seizes him, it throws him to the ground. He foams at the mouth, gnashes his teeth and becomes rigid. I

A Prescription for the Impotent Christian

asked your disciples to drive out the spirit, but they could not." "O unbelieving generation," Jesus replied, "how long shall I stay with you? How long shall I put up with you? Bring the boy to me." So they brought him. When the spirit saw Jesus, it immediately threw the boy into a convulsion. He fell to the ground and rolled around, foaming at the mouth. Jesus asked the boy's father, "How long has he been like this?" "From childhood," he answered. "It has often thrown him into fire or water to kill him. But if you can do anything, take pity on us and help us." "'If you can'?" said Jesus. "Everything is possible for him who believes." Immediately the boy's father exclaimed, "I do believe; help me overcome my unbelief!" When Jesus saw that a crowd was running to the scene, he rebuked the evil spirit. "You deaf and mute spirit," he said, "I command you, come out of him and never enter him again." The spirit shrieked, convulsed him violently and came out. The boy looked so much like a corpse that many said, "He's dead." But Jesus took him by the hand and lifted him to his feet, and he stood up. After Jesus had gone indoors, his disciples asked him privately, "Why couldn't we drive it out?" He replied, "This kind can come out only by *prayer and fasting."*

Do you have an urgent prayer need? Are you struggling with an addiction that keeps haunting you? Consider *fasting* as a way to energize your prayers. Practically speaking, what do we need to consider? First, your "heart" has to be right. The Pharisees fasted for the wrong reasons—God isn't interested, and won't bring about blessings, if you're "heart" isn't right.

Matthew 6:16-18 (NIV)

"When you fast, do not look somber as the hypocrites do, for they disfigure their faces to show men they are fasting. I tell you the truth, they have received their reward in full. But when you fast, put oil on your head and wash your face, so that it will not be obvious to men that you are fasting, but only to your Father, who is unseen; and your Father, who sees what is done in secret, will reward you.

Second, there are no rigid rules to follow. A fast can be any amount of time up to forty days. The most common are 1,3,or 7 days—longer is O.K. It can be a *total fast* (no food at all), or a *partial fast* (examples would be to stop drinking pop, or to eat only fruits and vegetables). It's very important to drink lots of water. I personally believe that there are some, yet undiscovered, health benefits to *fasting*—maybe related to cleansing impurities from our physical bodies (our fat stores can harbor many different chemicals). If you've been *fasting* for more than 3 days break your *fast* slowly— start with juice and advance your diet slowly. Is all this talk about fasting making you hungry? I promise you that *fasting* will open up a new dimension to your spiritual life—you may get physically hungry, but you'll hunger for more of God.

In summary, I challenge you to invest time in *both* areas of discipline. This small investment of time will pay out miraculous dividends in your life. Don't forget, "spiritual disciplines" first, then ask God to help you with the "physical disciplines." Consider *fasting* if God puts it on your "heart." I think this plan will free many from the burden of depression and chronic fatigue—not to mention, the whole host of other problems and addictions that plague our society. My challenge to you is to ***just start***. Pick a day (not "tomorrow" because it never comes), and a place, to begin your *daily meetings* with your Savior. He desires a relationship with you. He desires to free you from any addiction, bondage, or disease. He wants you to enter into "His workshop." It can be anywhere, but I believe the more secluded the better. It needs to be a place where you can audibly talk to God without being fearful of someone overhearing you. I think that a quiet, dark place is ideal. I like the idea of a "prayer closet"—maybe a chair in a walk-in closet. Rig up a small light so that you can read, study, and meditate on God's word. Listen for the small, still voice of the Holy Spirit. *Schedule* this time of solitude into your day—*this is vital*—this is why it's called *discipline*. Remember, **patient, sometimes painful, discipline—seasoned with grace**. God will reward your commitment to Him and you'll begin to gain strength each day. Ask God, in this time of solitude, to help you enhance and develop the other disciplines we've discussed: both "spiritual" (prayer, silence, reading/studying/meditating on God's Word, fellowship, and fasting) and "physical" (healthy diet, exercise, and rest/relaxation). It's important to come to God *daily*:

Isaiah 33:2 (NIV)
O LORD, be gracious to us; we long for you. Be our strength *every morning*, our salvation in time of distress.

Lamentations 3:22-26 (NIV)
Because of the LORD's great love we are not consumed, for his compassions never fail. They are new *every morning*; great is your faithfulness. I say to myself, "The LORD is my portion; therefore I will wait for him." The LORD is good to those whose hope is in him, to the one who seeks him; it is good to wait quietly for the salvation of the LORD.

Let God "cause it to grow." Don't rush God—let Him know that He's the most important thing in the world to you and that He is worthy of your time. You've entered His "workshop" and have begun to meet with Him daily. You'll feel stronger, more alive, but here's where most people fall short. They start the "race" in a sprint and then tire out and quit too early. Out of gas! We've talked a lot about disciplines—both "spiritual" and "physical." You may have actually begun to practice the disciplines on a regular basis, but now comes the hard part: *persistence* and *perseverance*! Don't make the mistake, however, of turning the "disciplines" into *laws*. Richard J. Foster said it best (again from his book, "Celebration of Discipline—the Path to Spiritual Growth")

"The spiritual disciplines are intended for our good. They are meant to bring the abundance of God into our lives. It is possible, however, to turn them into another set of soul-killing laws. Law-bound disciplines breathe death."

1 Thessalonians 5:23-24 (NIV)
May God himself, the God of peace, sanctify you through and through. May your whole spirit, soul and body be kept blameless at the coming of our Lord Jesus Christ. ***The one who calls you is faithful and he will do it.***

Let's move on to chapter 6 and learn the secret.

— Chapter 6 —

SLOW AND STEADY

How many times have you been inspired to begin some new diet or exercise program? You started strong, but in a week, or two, the enthusiasm waned and the end result—no real change. Why did you quit? Usually it's because you didn't see an *immediate* change. Without **persistence** and **perseverance** this is usually the outcome. The "disciplines" discussed in chapter 5 will not be maximally experienced without persistence and perseverance. We have to, not only enter God's workshop, but also, once in the workshop, begin to practice the "disciplines"—*consistently*, with persistence and perseverance. We need to *daily* meet with our God and, as time passes, we will begin to see changes taking place—*slowly*. Have you ever seen a plant actually growing? I didn't think so—I haven't either! We can appreciate growth after time has passed, or with time-lapse photography, but otherwise it is difficult to perceive changes occurring. We don't perceive changes in the growth of our children because we're with them daily. When someone, however, who has not seen them for a while visits, their usual comment is "My how they've grown." I hate to overuse the analogy but God has made it clear to me that our spiritual growth has many similarities to the physical process of growth—both with plants and animals. Occasionally we'll see growth spurts in our spiritual life as well, but the *real changes* take time. Slow and steady. God loves to see us be persistent! Jesus used a parable to prove his point:

Luke 18:1-8 (NIV)
Then Jesus told his disciples a parable to show them that they should always pray and *not give up*. He said: "In a certain town there was a judge who neither feared God nor cared about men. And there was a widow in that town who kept coming to him with the plea, 'Grant me justice against my adversary.' "For some time he refused. But finally he said to himself, 'Even though I don't fear God or care about men, yet because this widow keeps bothering me, I will see that she gets justice, so that she won't eventually wear me out with her coming!' And the Lord said, "Listen to what the unjust judge says. And will not God bring about justice for his chosen ones, who cry out to him day and night? Will he keep putting them off? I tell you, he will see that they get justice, and quickly. However, when the Son of Man comes, will he find faith on the earth?"

Persistence pays off! It is true, the "squeaky wheel gets the oil." Can we do anything to improve ourselves in this area? What can develop our perseverance?

James 1:2-4 (NIV)
Consider it pure joy, my brothers, whenever you face *trials* of many kinds, because you know that the *testing of your faith develops perseverance*. Perseverance must finish its work so that you may be mature and complete, not lacking anything.

Slow and Steady

I don't know if I like where this is going! The "testing of your faith" happens when you face "trials of many kinds." This *develops* our perseverance. I don't know about you, but I'm not too keen on praying for any "trials." What constitutes a "trial?" That's easy—anything that "tests your faith." I know—it seems like we're going in circles! How many days in your life can you remember where everything went "just right?" No bumps in the road, no waves in the sea. It doesn't usually happen does it? These are "trials"—anything that "rattles your cage." When you ask "why God?" it can be considered a "trial." Granted, there can be major storms, sometimes just a little wind and a few waves, or anything in between.

Matthew 8:24-27 (NIV)
Without warning, a furious storm came up on the lake, so that the waves swept over the boat. But Jesus was sleeping. The disciples went and woke him, saying, "Lord, save us! We're going to drown!" He replied, "You of little faith, why are you so afraid?" Then he got up and rebuked the winds and the waves, and it was completely calm. The men were amazed and asked, "What kind of man is this? Even the winds and the waves obey him!"

Notice that the storm can come up without warning. What's usually the outcome? It draws us closer to God. This is when we realize how inadequate we really are. We appreciate how *little* control we really have. It makes us hungry and we cry out and drop to our knees. If everything always went perfectly, it wouldn't take long before we would begin to feel self-sufficient, and then pride would enter in. Do we pray for "trials?" Absolutely not! They'll come regardless—because we live in a "sin filled, fallen world." What did Jesus say about them?

John 16:33 (NIV)
"I have told you these things, so that in me you may have peace. In this world you will have trouble. But take heart! I have overcome the world."

"Trials" usually cause us to be more dependent upon God. If we are more reliant upon Him, it will lead to intimacy in our relationship.

Satan is ultimately responsible for most of the problems we run into—directly, or indirectly. It gets back to our "sin nature", which, you remember, is battling with our "new nature."

James 1:13-15 (NIV)
When tempted, no one should say, "God is tempting me." For God cannot be tempted by evil, nor does he tempt anyone; but each one is tempted when, by his own evil desire, he is dragged away and enticed. Then, after desire has conceived, it gives birth to sin; and sin, when it is full-grown, gives birth to death.

Many times "trials" come about as a result of *our* own sin. Sin will *always* bring consequences—now, or later! Remember, if God says not to do something, it's not just because He wants to be a "killjoy." He knows that it will eventually hurt us in one way or another. Someone may have been a heavy "smoker and drinker" most of their life—perhaps they then experience the "instantaneous transformation." They have been "born again" spiritually and are a new creation in Christ. In spite of this spiritual rebirth, they may physically suffer from emphysema and liver disease. Why? Sin has consequences.

Sometimes "trials" arise from someone else's sin, and it ultimately affects you. A drunk driver kills someone you love. Need I say more?

Lastly, there can be "trials" for no apparent reason at all. The story of Job illustrates the classic example of someone experiencing "trials" for no apparent reason.

Job 1:1, 3b (NIV)
In the land of Uz there lived a man whose name was Job. This man was blameless and upright; he feared God and shunned evil. He was the greatest man among all the people of the East.

Job 1:8-12 (NIV)
Then the LORD said to Satan, "Have you considered my servant Job? There is no one on earth like him; he is blameless and upright, a man who fears God and shuns evil." "Does Job fear God for nothing?" Satan replied. "Have you not put a hedge around him and his household and everything he has? You have blessed the work of his hands, so that his flocks and herds are spread throughout the land. But stretch out your hand and strike everything he has, and he will surely curse you to your face." The LORD said to Satan, "Very well, then, everything he has is in your hands, but on the man himself do not lay a finger." Then Satan went out from the presence of the LORD.

Even God was proud of Job! What happened? Satan was given permission to pound Job with one "trial" after another. Ultimately, Job persevered under trial and God, once again, made a spectacle of Satan. If you are ever overwhelmed by a "trial" your going through, read the Book of Job. He lost his wife and children, all his possessions, and even his health. Yet he did not blame God.

Job 1:20-22 (NIV)
At this, Job got up and tore his robe and shaved his head. Then he fell to the ground in worship and said: "Naked I came from my mother's womb, and naked I will depart. The LORD gave and the LORD has taken away; may the name of the LORD be praised."

In all this, Job did not sin by charging God with wrongdoing.

Did God allow the trials? Yes, and after He saw Job through them, He blessed Job far beyond what He had before.

James 5:10-11 (NIV)
Brothers, as an example of patience in the face of suffering, take the prophets who spoke in the name of the Lord. As you know, we consider blessed those who have persevered. You have heard of Job's perseverance and have seen what the Lord finally brought about. The Lord is full of compassion and mercy.

You have to remember—God sees the "big picture." He knows how the story is going to unfold. It gets back to the issue of *trust*.

Proverbs 3:5-6 (NIV)
Trust in the LORD with all your heart and lean not on your own understanding; in all your ways acknowledge him, and he will make your paths straight.

Slow and Steady

Trust God's understanding—not your own. He knows what's best and we *have* to believe this. Commit the above verse to memory. I promise that you'll use it over and over again. God wants us to have peace in our lives. He doesn't want us to be "tossed back and forth by the waves."

Isaiah 26:3 (NIV)
You will keep in perfect peace him whose mind is steadfast, because he trusts in you.

What should you do when the "trials" arise? How did Jesus respond to Satan in the wilderness? By quoting the "Word of God." I believe the next few verses are worth committing to memory—to use whenever you're in need. God can be trusted!

Isaiah 41:10 (NIV)
So do not fear, for I am with you; do not be dismayed, for I am your God. I will strengthen you and help you; I will uphold you with my righteous right hand.

Philippians 4:13 (NIV)
I can do everything through him who gives me strength.

Philippians 4:19 (NIV)
And my God will meet all your needs according to his glorious riches in Christ Jesus.

Romans 8:28 (NIV)
And we know that in all things God works for the good of those who love him, who have been called according to his purpose.

A Prescription for the Impotent Christian

   Obviously, there are many more in the Bible, but I believe that these are some of the most foundational. They all speak to the fact that God is to be our source of strength and power, our place of refuge in the "storm." What if you pray for something and God doesn't answer your prayer? Always remember that last verse above—Romans 8:28—trust that God knows what He's doing. It may not make any sense at all in *your* mind.
   I have two different stories to tell regarding "trust during trials." The first has a happy ending, not so with the second.
   One day, at work in the Emergency Room, a "code blue" was called over the P.A. system. I responded to the call only to discover that a man in his 50's had experienced a cardiorespiratory arrest. He had been in the hospital for treatment of a blood clot in his leg. Our code team tried to resuscitate him, but our efforts failed and he died. I had never met this man before. The next day, I inadvertently ran into the pathologist who had just performed this man's autopsy. He told me that he had died from a massive blood clot to the lung but they had also, unexpectedly, found lung cancer. He commented that his death was "probably a blessing in disguise." I agreed—he would very likely have experienced a slow, painful death, in a few short months. Instead, he died very quickly and did not suffer at all. My thoughts were then interrupted by a nurse telling me about my next patient—a woman complaining of anxiousness and "Oh, by the way, her husband just died yesterday." This was the man's wife! I felt very inadequate, and frustrated, at that instant. I was powerless. What could I possibly offer this poor woman? *There was nothing that I could do.* Then I heard God's voice speak into my spirit, "Tell her what the pathologist told you. I want her to know." I was obedient, and after introducing myself, I simply told her the same story that I told you. She began to sob and we cried together. She told me that she now had peace about his death and that she knew that God was

going to use the situation to glorify Himself. Wow! What a feeling! God had used me as His voice and I was "flying high." God used me to give this woman *just enough* to show her that He was still in control and that He knew what He was doing. *God can be trusted.* Notice, however, that there was still a "trial"—the man died, and his family grieved. Interestingly, he was the pastor of a small Bible Church in a nearby town. He was a "born-again Christian" and I knew, as did his wife, that he had gone "home" to be with Jesus.

1 Corinthians 15:55 (NIV)
"Where, O death, is your victory? Where, O death, is your sting?"

We can always trust that, as believers, God knows what He's doing. The "trials" we're experiencing may not make any sense of all—it may even take years before we understand it. We may never understand it until we leave this earthly life.

I have another story that, unfortunately, had a different outcome. This one was heard secondhand and is not my own personal experience, but it also illustrates the importance of trusting God in *all* circumstances.

A wonderful Christian family was blessed with a newborn baby daughter. She was beautiful and was her mother's pride and joy. When she turned two years old, however, she began to look pale and was losing weight. Mom took her to the doctor and a blood test revealed leukemia. After further tests, the doctors told the parents that it was a very aggressive type and that she probably wouldn't live more than six months. What would your reaction be? How would you respond to God about this one? Obviously, the parents were distraught, but mother was also very angry. She demanded that God heal her daughter and she swore that if God let her daughter die she would never forgive Him for it! Over the next few weeks, a medical miracle occurred. The leukemia, for no apparent reason, went into remission. The small child once again became healthy! But wait, the story doesn't end here. The next few years went well, but then came the turbulent teenage years. The daughter became very rebellious against her parents and caused them much pain. She also rejected their Christian faith and became heavily involved in drugs, and the occult. Then, on her 18th birthday, she was tragically killed in an automobile accident. She died and had never made a commitment to Jesus Christ. She had not been "born again." There are several things to consider about this story. Jesus said:

Mark 8:36-37 (NIV)
What good is it for a man to gain the whole world, yet forfeit his soul? Or what can a man give in exchange for his soul?

If the daughter had died from leukemia when she was two years old, she would have spent *eternity* with Jesus, and her parents, in Heaven. Did God know what the ultimate outcome of her life was going to be? You bet. Was God, in reality, attempting to rescue this girl's soul from eternal hell by taking her at an early age—before the "age of accountability?" It's possible. It took years before the final outcome of the story made any sense. Always remember, that God can take the worst of *any situation* and make good come out of it.

No discussion of "trials" would be complete without examining the concept of *suffering*. As stated before, " trials" can come in all shapes and sizes—minor, major, long, short, etc. Suffering is *always* a "trial." Not all "trials" involve suffering. Suffering can be:

- Self-inflicted—a result, or consequence, of our own sin.
- Inflicted by another—directly, or indirectly, a consequence of someone else's sin.
- God inflicted/God allowed

We've already briefly discussed the first two, but what about that last one? This is a hot topic of debate. Does God inflict suffering? I think there is ample scriptural evidence for this. There are numerous instances in the Old Testament where God *directly* brought about judgment (suffering) on people. The ten plagues used by God to convince Pharaoh to let the Hebrews leave Egypt are a classic example. In the New Testament, consider the story of Ananias and Sapphira.

Acts 5:1-11 (NIV)

Now a man named Ananias, together with his wife Sapphira, also sold a piece of property. With his wife's full knowledge he kept back part of the money for himself, but brought the rest and put it at the apostles' feet. Then Peter said, "Ananias, how is it that Satan has so filled your heart that you have lied to the Holy Spirit and have kept for yourself some of the money you received for the land? Didn't it belong to you before it was sold? And after it was sold, wasn't the money at your disposal? What made you think of doing such a thing? You have not lied to men but to God." When Ananias heard this, he fell down and died. And great fear seized all who heard what had happened. Then the young men came forward, wrapped up his body, and carried him out and buried him. About three hours later his wife came in, not knowing what had happened. Peter asked her, "Tell me, is this the price you and Ananias got for the land?" "Yes," she said, "that is the price." Peter said to her, "How could you agree to test the Spirit of the Lord? Look! The feet of the men who buried your husband are at the door, and they will carry you out also." At that moment she fell down at his feet and died. Then the young men came in and, finding her dead, carried her out and buried her beside her husband. Great fear seized the whole church and all who heard about these events.

I've noticed that many times "God inflicted suffering" is related to judgment. I believe that most suffering is also a result of our "sin filled, fallen world." God may not actually be the direct cause, but He allows it. It may be used for *discipline*. It may be used as a "wake-up call." I believe that Satan is the author of the majority of all the suffering that goes on. God, however, is an expert at taking Satan's apparent victories and turning them into situations that bring glory to Himself.

Suffering can involve body, soul, or spirit.
We are all familiar with physical suffering—illness in our *bodies*—chronic pain from cancer, arthritis, and a multitude of other painful diseases. An interesting subset would be physical suffering inflicted as a result of *persecution*. We'll talk more about this a little later in the chapter. The apostles were very familiar with this form of suffering.

Acts 5:40b-42 (NIV)
They called the apostles in and had them flogged. Then they ordered them not to speak in the name of Jesus, and let them go. The apostles left the Sanhedrin, rejoicing because they had been counted worthy of suffering disgrace for the Name. Day after day, in the temple courts and from house

to house, they never stopped teaching and proclaiming the good news that Jesus is the Christ.

Suffering can involve our *souls*—our mind, will, and emotions. Depression, grief related to the death or illness of a loved one, and verbal abuse from a spouse are a few examples. There are many, many more.

There can also be suffering in our *spirit*.

Ephesians 4:30 (NIV)
And do not grieve the Holy Spirit of God, with whom you were sealed for the day of redemption.

This occurs when we are living outside of the "Will of God." Unconfessed sins, secret sins, anything that breaks fellowship with God. We'll discuss this more in the next chapter. How does this all fit together? Suffering affects *all* in the human race—Christian or non-Christian. Many times it can involve body, soul, and spirit, simultaneously. **I believe that it is God's will for every Christian to *ultimately* be delivered from their suffering.** Notice, however, that I said *ultimately*. Some are delivered (healed) instantaneously. Other times it may take days, months, or even years. Some aren't delivered until the death of their physical body.

Jesus performed many miracles when He walked on the earth. Multitudes were healed and usually it was *instantaneous* healing.

Luke 8:43-44 (NIV)
And a woman was there who had been subject to bleeding for twelve years, but no one could heal her. She came up behind him and touched the edge of his cloak, and immediately her bleeding stopped.

Does this still happen today? Yes it does! The Bible is clear that some "believers" have been given the *gift* of miracles and healing. God works *through* these people to bring about miracles and healing.

1 Corinthians 12:27-31 (NIV)
> Now you are the body of Christ, and each one of you is a part of it. And in the church God has appointed first of all apostles, second prophets, third teachers, *then workers of miracles, also those having gifts of healing,* those able to help others, those with gifts of administration, and those speaking in different kinds of tongues. Are all apostles? Are all prophets? Are all teachers? Do all work miracles? Do all have gifts of healing? Do all speak in tongues? Do all interpret? But eagerly desire the greater gifts.

Instantaneous healings are awesome, but, honestly, they don't happen as often as we would like them to. How else does God bring about healing and deliverance? *Time*—maybe short, maybe long. I believe that God will deliver many from illness and suffering *over a period of time*. God has built "healing" into our physical bodies. It's amazing to watch how our bodies can heal themselves. This healing and regeneration goes on constantly. You've heard it said, "Time heals all wounds"; I believe that there's wisdom in this statement. This is where physicians fit into the picture. God can miraculously heal anyone, but I believe that the avenue we should pursue, *if instantaneous healing doesn't occur,* is to see a physician. God commonly works through physicians to bring about healing. *Ideally*, it should be combined with prayer.

Slow and Steady

James 5:14-16 (NIV)
Is any one of you sick? He should call the elders of the church to pray over him and anoint him with oil in the name of the Lord. And the prayer offered in faith will make the sick person well; the Lord will raise him up. If he has sinned, he will be forgiven. Therefore confess your sins to each other and pray for each other so that you may be healed. The prayer of a righteous man is powerful and effective.

Remember, Luke was a physician himself. Did Jesus make any comments about doctors?

Luke 5:3-321 (NIV)
Jesus answered them, "It is not the healthy who need a doctor, but the sick. I have not come to call the righteous, but sinners to repentance."

Look at this quick story in the Old Testament.

2 Kings 20:1-7 (NIV)
In those days Hezekiah became ill and was at the point of death. The prophet Isaiah son of Amoz went to him and said, "This is what the LORD says: Put your house in order, because you are going to die; you will not recover." Hezekiah turned his face to the wall and prayed to the LORD, "Remember, O LORD, how I have walked before you faithfully and with wholehearted devotion and have done what is good in your eyes." And Hezekiah wept bitterly. Before Isaiah had left the middle court, the word of the LORD came to him: "Go back and tell Hezekiah, the leader of my people, 'This is what the LORD, the God of your father

A Prescription for the Impotent Christian

> David, says: I have heard your prayer and seen your tears; I will heal you. On the third day from now you will go up to the temple of the LORD. I will add fifteen years to your life. And I will deliver you and this city from the hand of the king of Assyria. I will defend this city for my sake and for the sake of my servant David.'" Then Isaiah said, *"Prepare a poultice of figs." They did so and applied it to the boil, and he recovered.*

This was a situation where God was responsible for the healing but used medicine to facilitate it (a poultice of figs). As I said before, I believe that many of the illnesses Americans suffer from would vanish with proper exercise, diet, and rest—*especially* if it's combined with the practice of the "spiritual disciplines" as well. Please remember, however, not all receive healing from their illnesses. Many people leave our modern-day "healing crusades" not healed, and they are discouraged. Some "believers", many of whom had more faith then I'll ever know, were not delivered from their suffering until the death of their physical body. How about some examples. Elisha was a mighty prophet of God in the Old Testament.

2 Kings 13:14a (NIV)
Now Elisha was suffering from the illness from which he died.

Another classic example involved the apostle Paul.

2 Corinthians 12:7-10 (NIV)
To keep me from becoming conceited because of these surpassingly great revelations, there was given me a *thorn in my flesh*, a messenger of Satan, to torment me. Three times I pleaded with the Lord

to take it away from me. But he said to me, "My grace is sufficient for you, for my power is made perfect in weakness." Therefore I will boast all the more gladly about my weaknesses, so that Christ's power may rest on me. That is why, for Christ's sake, I delight in weaknesses, in insults, in hardships, in persecutions, in difficulties. For when I am weak, then I am strong.

Scholars think Paul's "thorn" may have been a physical problem—maybe a problem with his vision. Note, however, that God *refused* to heal him. What did God tell Paul? *"My grace is sufficient for you for my power is made perfect in weakness."* I believe that *grace* is God's answer for helping us to cope with illness and suffering. Once we accept that we are powerless to do anything about it then God will either heal us (instantaneously, or over time) or give us the ability to deal with it! Just when you think you can't take it anymore God steps in and carries you. This *grace* is intimately tied in with God's *mercy*.

We've talked a lot about suffering, but I want to finish on this theme with a discussion of a very special subset of suffering—*persecution*. I believe that this particular type of suffering carries with it a special blessing. This is where, I believe, we can really see God's *grace* in action. What does Scripture say about this type of suffering?

Philippians 1:29-30 (NIV)
For it has been granted to you on behalf of Christ not only to believe on him, but *also to suffer for him*, since you are going through the same struggle you saw I had, and now hear that I still have.

2 Timothy 3:10-12 (NIV)
You, however, know all about my teaching, my

way of life, my purpose, faith, patience, love, endurance, persecutions, sufferings—what kinds of things happened to me in Antioch, Iconium and Lystra, the persecutions I endured. Yet the Lord rescued me from all of them. *In fact, everyone who wants to live a godly life in Christ Jesus will be persecuted.*

John 15:18-20 (NIV)
"If the world hates you, keep in mind that it hated me first. If you belonged to the world, it would love you as its own. As it is, you do not belong to the world, but I have chosen you out of the world. That is why the world hates you. Remember the words I spoke to you: 'No servant is greater than his master.' *If they persecuted me, they will persecute you also.* If they obeyed my teaching, they will obey yours also.

Matthew 5:11-12 (NIV)
"Blessed are you when people insult you, persecute you and falsely say all kinds of evil against you because of me. Rejoice and be glad, because great is your reward in heaven, for in the same way they persecuted the prophets who were before you.

It seems like maybe we should be worried, doesn't it? Persecution seems to be *inevitable* for the Christian. Notice, however, that it does carry with it a very special reward (blessing) in Heaven. Virtually all of the apostles died torturous deaths as martyrs for Jesus Christ. Remember all of the first century Christians who died at the hands of the Romans—many were fed to the lions! There have been more people martyred for Jesus Christ *in this century alone* then in all the other centuries combined. How do these people make it through a "trial" like this? I sincerely believe that it is a "God thing"—His *grace* is sufficient. Look at the story of Stephen, the first Christian martyr.

Acts 6:8-12 (NIV)
> Now Stephen, a man full of God's grace and power, did great wonders and miraculous signs among the people. Opposition arose, however, from members of the Synagogue of the Freedmen (as it was called)—Jews of Cyrene and Alexandria as well as the provinces of Cilicia and Asia. These men began to argue with Stephen, but they could not stand up against his wisdom or the Spirit by whom he spoke. Then they secretly persuaded some men to say, "We have heard Stephen speak words of blasphemy against Moses and against God." So they stirred up the people and the elders and the teachers of the law. They seized Stephen and brought him before the Sanhedrin.

Stephen then proceeded to give them the "sermon of their life." You can read it in Acts: Chapter 7. Notice how it ends.

Acts 7:54-60 (NIV)
> When they heard this, they were furious and gnashed their teeth at him. But Stephen, full of the Holy Spirit, looked up to heaven and saw the glory of God, and Jesus standing at the right hand of God. "Look," he said, "I see heaven open and the Son of Man standing at the right hand of God." At this they covered their ears and, yelling at the top of their voices, they all rushed at him, dragged him out of the city and began to stone him. Meanwhile, the witnesses laid their clothes at the feet of a young man named Saul. While they were stoning

him, Stephen prayed, "Lord Jesus, receive my spirit." Then he fell on his knees and cried out, "Lord, do not hold this sin against them." *When he had said this, he fell asleep.*

Notice that Stephen asked God to forgive them! Wow! Then God helped to deliver Stephen by allowing him to "go to sleep." God spared him from the painful suffering that would have undoubtedly occurred. *No "born-again" Christian will ever be martyred apart from God's will.* He is in control and if this is His will—His choice for your life—then He will graciously equip you with the ability to be able to do it.

Rachel Scott and Cassie Bernal were two young women who professed their Savior, *unashamedly.* You will recall they died in the Columbine massacre. They died as martyrs for their God—apparently asked the question "Do you still believe in God?" Their answer, "You know that I do." God has since used their deaths to bring literally millions to a saving knowledge of Jesus Christ.

Jim Elliot, a famous missionary to the Auca Indians of Ecuador, was also martyred for his faith. He said, "He is no fool who gives what he cannot keep to gain what he can never lose."

How did we get here? We were talking about *persistence* and *perseverance.* "Trials" and "suffering" test our faith and develop our perseverance. As a result, our faith grows.

2 Thessalonians 1:3-5 (NIV)

> We ought always to thank God for you, brothers, and rightly so, because your faith is growing more and more, and the love every one of you has for each other is increasing. Therefore, among God's churches we boast about your perseverance and faith in all the persecutions and trials you are endur-

ing. All this is evidence that God's judgment is right, and as a result you will be counted worthy of the kingdom of God, for which you are suffering.

Romans 5:1-5 (NIV)
Therefore, since we have been justified through faith, we have peace with God through our Lord Jesus Christ, through whom we have gained access by faith into this grace in which we now stand. And we rejoice in the hope of the glory of God. Not only so, but we also rejoice in our sufferings, because we know that *suffering produces perseverance; perseverance, character; and character, hope.* And hope does not disappoint us, because God has poured out his love into our hearts by the Holy Spirit, whom he has given us.

We now understand that persistence and perseverance are developed by our "trials" and "sufferings." We should be careful, however, to examine the "trial" and make certain it's not a result of our own sin. Make certain that you have no unconfessed sin in your life: an unforgiving spirit, an addiction, or some other problem that is hindering your relationship with God. What should you do if you do?

2 Chronicles 7:14 (NIV)
...if my people, who are called by my name, will humble themselves and pray and seek my face and turn from their wicked ways, then will I hear from heaven and will forgive their sin and will heal their land.

Remember, it's all about growth.

Hebrews 6:1 (NIV)
Therefore let us leave the elementary teachings about Christ and go on to maturity…

Ephesians 4:14-16 (NIV)
Then we will no longer be infants, tossed back and forth by the waves, and blown here and there by every wind of teaching and by the cunning and craftiness of men in their deceitful scheming. Instead, speaking the truth in love, *we will in all things grow up into him* who is the Head, that is, Christ. From him the whole body, joined and held together by every supporting ligament, grows and builds itself up in love, as each part does its work.

2 Peter 3:17-18 (NIV)
Therefore, dear friends, since you already know this, be on your guard so that you may not be carried away by the error of lawless men and fall from your secure position. *But grow in the grace and knowledge of our Lord and Savior Jesus Christ.* To him be glory both now and forever! Amen.

We start our new life at the "instantaneous transformation." We are "born again" and we are "new creatures in Christ." We are called infants, babies.

1 Peter 2:2-3 (NIV)
Like newborn babies, crave pure spiritual milk, so that by it you may grow up in your salvation, now that you have tasted that the Lord is good.

As we grow, however, we need to "advance our diet" to solid food.

Slow and Steady

Hebrews 5:11-14 (NIV)
We have much to say about this, but it is hard to explain because you are slow to learn. In fact, though by this time you ought to be teachers, you need someone to teach you the elementary truths of God's word all over again. You need milk, not solid food! Anyone who lives on milk, being still an infant, is not acquainted with the teaching about righteousness. But solid food is for the mature, who by constant use have trained themselves to distinguish good from evil.

1 Corinthians 3:1-3a (NIV)
Brothers, I could not address you as spiritual but as worldly—mere infants in Christ. I gave you milk, not solid food, for you were not yet ready for it. Indeed, you are still not ready. You are still worldly.

How do we grow? Enter "God's workshop", practice the "spiritual and physical disciplines", and *God causes us to grow!* Growth is God's responsibility!

1 Corinthians 3:6-10 (NIV)
I planted the seed, Apollos watered it, but *God made it grow*. So neither he who plants nor he who waters is anything, but only God, who makes things grow. The man who plants and the man who waters have one purpose, and each will be rewarded according to his own labor. For we are God's fellow workers; you are God's field, God's building. By the grace God has given me, I laid a foundation as an expert builder, and someone else is building on it. But each one should be careful how he builds.

A Prescription for the Impotent Christian

I stumbled into what I thought, at first, seemed like a contradiction. All of this talk about growth! Doesn't the Bible say we're to "stand firm?" Look at these verses.

Luke 21:19 (NIV)
By *standing firm* you will gain life.

1 Corinthians 15:58 (NIV)
Therefore, my dear brothers, *stand firm*. Let nothing move you. Always give yourselves fully to the work of the Lord, because you know that your labor in the Lord is not in vain.

Galatians 5:1 (NIV)
It is for freedom that Christ has set us free. *Stand firm*, then, and do not let yourselves be burdened again by a yoke of slavery.

James 5:7-8 (NIV)
Be patient, then, brothers, until the Lord's coming. See how the farmer waits for the land to yield its valuable crop and how patient he is for the autumn and spring rains. You too, be patient and *stand firm*, because the Lord's coming is near.

How can we "stand firm" and yet "grow" at the same time? Think, once again, about a plant. It "grows" best when it is "standing firm"—a solid root structure anchors it in place. This allows for the best growth, because the root system provides a way for nourishment to get to the plant. Satan is constantly trying to uproot us!

1 Peter 5:8-9 (NIV)
Be self-controlled and alert. Your enemy the devil prowls around like a roaring lion looking for

Slow and Steady

someone to devour. Resist him, standing firm in the faith, because you know that your brothers throughout the world are undergoing the same kind of sufferings.

1 Corinthians 10:12-13 (NIV)
So, if you think you are standing firm, be careful that you don't fall! No temptation has seized you except what is common to man. And God is faithful; he will not let you be tempted beyond what you can bear. But when you are tempted, he will also provide a way out so that you can stand up under it.

So, if God is responsible for our "growth", what about our ability to "stand firm?"

2 Corinthians 1:21-22 (NIV)
Now *it is God who makes both us and you stand firm in Christ.* He anointed us, set his seal of ownership on us, and put his Spirit in our hearts as a deposit, guaranteeing what is to come.

Exodus 14:13-14 (NIV)
Moses answered the people, "Do not be afraid. *Stand firm and you will see the deliverance the LORD will bring you today.* The Egyptians you see today you will never see again. The LORD will fight for you; you need only to be still."

It really is true! The battle is the Lord's. He is ultimately responsible for our "standing firm" *and* "growing." If this is true, why do we so often not experience it?

A Prescription for the Impotent Christian

Ephesians 6:10-18 (NIV)
Finally, be strong in the Lord and in his mighty power. Put on the full armor of God so that you can take your stand against the devil's schemes. For our struggle is not against flesh and blood, but against the rulers, against the authorities, against the powers of this dark world and against the spiritual forces of evil in the heavenly realms. Therefore put on the full armor of God, so that when the day of evil comes, you may be able to stand your ground, and after you have done everything, to stand. Stand firm then, with the belt of truth buckled around your waist, with the breastplate of righteousness in place, and with your feet fitted with the readiness that comes from the gospel of peace. In addition to all this, take up the shield of faith, with which you can extinguish all the flaming arrows of the evil one. Take the helmet of salvation and the sword of the Spirit, which is the word of God. And pray in the Spirit on all occasions with all kinds of prayers and requests. With this in mind, be alert and always keep on praying for all the saints.

How can we put on God's *full armor* to protect ourselves against Satan's attacks? By getting into "God's workshop" and practicing the "disciplines!" I don't imagine that the knights of the Middle Ages could just slip into their armor in a few minutes. I would envision that it was a time-consuming task. I also expect that it couldn't be done alone. It will take an investment of time for you, as well, to put on God's armor. It will be helpful to get someone else to assist you (i.e. pray with you, and for you). Remember, there is power in numbers, and *fellowship* is also one of the "disciplines."

In summary, God rewards persistence and perseverance. Our perseverance, and faith, is developed, and strengthened, through "trials" and "sufferings"—an inevitable part of our human existence. God promises, however, to be our source of strength and power. *He* is responsible for us "standing firm" and "growing." This is a *lifelong process* (only God knows how long) and it is by nature "slow and steady." It has been said, "There are no shortcuts to anywhere worth going." This is especially true in our Christian "walk." Remember, this is all part of the "gradual transformation." The "religious" word you may have heard is *sanctification*—becoming more and more like Christ.

1 Peter 1:3-9 (NIV)
Praise be to the God and Father of our Lord Jesus Christ! In his great mercy he has given us new birth into a living hope through the resurrection of Jesus Christ from the dead, and into an inheritance that can never perish, spoil or fade—kept in heaven for you, who through faith are shielded by God's power until the coming of the salvation that is ready to be revealed in the last time. In this you greatly rejoice, though now for a little while you may have had to suffer grief in all kinds of trials. These have come so that your faith—of greater worth than gold, which perishes even though refined by fire—may be proved genuine and may result in praise, glory and honor when Jesus Christ is revealed. Though you have not seen him, you love him; and even though you do not see him now, you believe in him and are filled with an inexpressible and glorious joy, for you are receiving the goal of your faith, the salvation of your souls.

A Prescription for the Impotent Christian

The apostle Paul talked about the "gradual transformation" as a "race."

1 Corinthians 9:24-27 (NIV)
Do you not know that in a race all the runners run, but only one gets the prize? Run in such a way as to get the prize. Everyone who competes in the games goes into strict training. They do it to get a crown that will not last; but we do it to get a crown that will last forever. Therefore I do not run like a man running aimlessly; I do not fight like a man beating the air. No, I beat my body and make it my slave so that after I have preached to others, I myself will not be disqualified for the prize.

We should run the race "in such a way as to get the prize." Our goal should be to *run hard and finish strong*—we are called to "finish the race."

Acts 20:24 (NIV)
However, I consider my life worth nothing to me, if only I may *finish the race* and complete the task the Lord Jesus has given me—the task of testifying to the gospel of God's grace.

There has already been a winner of the race—Jesus Christ! He is the champion!
When Paul was in jail, awaiting his execution, he talked about having finished the "race."

2 Timothy 4:6-8 (NIV)
For I am already being poured out like a drink offering, and the time has come for my departure. I have fought the good fight, I have finished the race, I have kept the faith. Now there is in store for

me the crown of righteousness, which the Lord, the righteous Judge, will award to me on that day—and not only to me, but also to all who have longed for his appearing.

Yes, Paul finished the race, as have multiplied millions of others, and they are cheering us onto the finish line!

Hebrews 12:1-3 (NIV)
Therefore, since we are surrounded by such a great cloud of witnesses, let us throw off everything that hinders and the sin that so easily entangles, and let us run with perseverance the race marked out for us. Let us fix our eyes on Jesus, the author and perfecter of our faith, who for the joy set before him endured the cross, scorning its shame, and sat down at the right hand of the throne of God. Consider him who endured such opposition from sinful men, so that you will not grow weary and lose heart.

Remember, there is "no shortcut—no quick fix." Keep your focus on Jesus Christ.

2 Corinthians 4:16-18 (NIV)
Therefore we do not lose heart. Though outwardly we are wasting away, yet inwardly we are being renewed day by day. For our light and momentary troubles are achieving for us an eternal glory that far outweighs them all. So we fix our eyes not on what is seen, but on what is unseen. For what is seen is temporary, but what is unseen is eternal.

A Prescription for the Impotent Christian

Eternity is really all that matters. How close is the finish line? Only God knows that. My hope is that you now realize that God is able to give you all that you need to finish the race strong—to achieve Christ-like perfection. Give Jesus a chance.

John 15:11 (NIV)
I have told you this so that my joy may be in you and that your joy may be complete.

On to the last chapter!

— Chapter 7 —

AM I PERFECT YET?

Have you seen the bumper sticker "Please be patient—God isn't finished with me yet?" This brings the inevitable question—when will God be finished with me? When will I be perfect like Jesus Christ? I tried to show in chapter 6 that the changes taking place in the "gradual transformation" are *slow and steady*. We are "running the race" and our goal is to cross the finish line. Only God knows when each one of us will cross the finish line. The apostle Paul put it into perspective.

> **Philippians 3:4b-14(NIV)**
> If anyone else thinks he has reasons to put confidence in the flesh, I have more: circumcised on the eighth day, of the people of Israel, of the tribe of Benjamin, a Hebrew of Hebrews; in regard to the law, a Pharisee; as for zeal, persecuting the church; as for legalistic righteousness, faultless. But whatever was to my profit I now consider loss for the sake of Christ. What is more, I consider everything a loss compared to the surpassing greatness of knowing Christ Jesus my Lord, for whose sake I have lost all things. I consider them rubbish, that I may gain Christ and be found in

him, not having a righteousness of my own that comes from the law, but that which is through faith in Christ—the righteousness that comes from God and is by faith. I want to know Christ and the power of his resurrection and the fellowship of sharing in his sufferings, becoming like him in his death, and so, somehow, to attain to the resurrection from the dead. *Not that I have already obtained all this, or have already been made perfect, but I press on to take hold of that for which Christ Jesus took hold of me.* Brothers, I do not consider myself yet to have taken hold of it. But one thing I do: Forgetting what is behind and straining toward what is ahead, I press on toward the goal to win the prize for which God has called me heavenward in Christ Jesus.

Paul had good reason to have confidence in himself. In the Jewish culture, he was "at the top of his game." He was willing, however, to give it all up for Christ. Why? Because he wanted the following:

- To know Christ as his Lord
- To gain Christ's righteousness by faith
- To have Christ's power
- To share in Christ's sufferings
- To be like Christ in his death
- To attain resurrection from the dead

He knew he wasn't there yet! Only God knew when it would be Paul's time. What was Paul to do? What should we do? Forget about the past—it's over—"strain" toward what is ahead. Press on toward the goal (the finish line) so that we can win the "prize." Keep plugging away—*slow and steady*. I believe that the race isn't finished, and we will not be "made perfect", until we experience the death of our physical body. What happens then? Mankind has been "dying" to know the answer to this one since the dawn of creation. Remember, when our physical body dies the soul departs. What happens to our soul? If we have been "born-again" spiritually (i.e. the "instantaneous transformation"), then our soul/spirit will be immediately taken to be in God's presence in Heaven. If any individual dies *without* having accepted God's free "gift" of eternal life, their soul, unfortunately, goes to Hell. Hell is a place, as we've already discussed, intended for Satan and his demons. It involves torment and separation from God.

One day there will be a *bodily* resurrection, for both "believers" and "unbelievers."

Acts 24:15 (NIV)
...and I have the same hope in God as these men, that there will be a resurrection of both the righteous and the wicked.

It will be an exciting time for the "born again" Christian. Our soul/spirit will be reunited with our newly transformed body.

1 Corinthians 15:12-14 (NIV)
But if it is preached that Christ has been raised from the dead, how can some of you say that there is no resurrection of the dead? If there is no resurrection of the dead, then not even Christ has been raised. And if Christ has not been raised, our preaching is useless and so is your faith.

Philippians 3:20-21 (NIV)
But our citizenship is in heaven. And we eagerly await a Savior from there, the Lord Jesus Christ,

who, by the power that enables him to bring everything under his control, will transform our lowly bodies so that they will be like his glorious body.

We will not be bound by time. We will be eternal beings. We will have glorious new bodies. We will live and reign with Christ forever!

Has the resurrection taken place yet? No—it is an event *yet to come*. The resurrection occurs for " believers" that have died (the Bible says "fallen asleep"), and "believers" still alive on earth at that time, at an event called the "rapture" of the church and Paul describes it in the following verse:

1 Thessalonians 4:13-18 (NIV)
Brothers, we do not want you to be ignorant about those who fall asleep, or to grieve like the rest of men, who have no hope. We believe that Jesus died and rose again and so we believe that God will bring with Jesus those who have fallen asleep in him. According to the Lord's own word, we tell you that we who are still alive, who are left till the coming of the Lord, will certainly not precede those who have fallen asleep. For the Lord himself will come down from heaven, with a loud command, with the voice of the archangel and with the trumpet call of God, and the dead in Christ will rise first. After that, we who are still alive and are left will be caught up together with them in the clouds to meet the Lord in the air. And so we will be with the Lord forever. Therefore encourage each other with these words.

Will there be a bodily resurrection for "unbelievers?" Yes. It's called the "Great White Throne" judgment. It occurs at a later time.

Revelation 20:11-15 (NIV)
Then I saw a great white throne and him who was seated on it. Earth and sky fled from his presence, and there was no place for them. And I saw the dead, great and small, standing before the throne, and books were opened. Another book was opened, which is the book of life. The dead were judged according to what they had done as recorded in the books. The sea gave up the dead that were in it, and death and Hades gave up the dead that were in them, and each person was judged according to what he had done. Then death and Hades were thrown into the lake of fire. The lake of fire is the second death. If anyone's name was not found written in the book of life, he was thrown into the lake of fire.

Is your name written in the "Book of Life?" If you have experienced the "instantaneous transformation" then it is!

Doesn't the Bible talk about "prizes" and "rewards?" Yes! There will be *judgment* for both "believers" and "unbelievers." All "believers" will be rewarded for "good works" done while they were present on this earth.

1 Corinthians 3:10-15(NIV)
By the grace God has given me, I laid a foundation as an expert builder, and someone else is building on it. But each one should be careful how he builds. For no one can lay any foundation other than the one already laid, which is Jesus Christ. If any man builds on this foundation using gold, silver, costly stones, wood, hay or straw, his work will be shown for what it is, because the Day will bring it to light. It will be revealed with fire, and the fire will test the quality of each man's work. If

what he has built survives, he will receive his *reward*. If it is burned up, he will suffer loss; he himself will be saved, but only as one escaping through the flames.

Don't ever forget that our "good works" have nothing to do with the salvation of our souls—salvation, my friend, is a "gift!" Eternal life is a free "gift" provided by Christ's death and resurrection—the "instantaneous transformation." It is by way of the "gradual transformation" that we fulfill the purpose and destiny that God had prepared *in advance* for our lives.

We know that our salvation is by grace, not by works.

Ephesians 2:8-10 (NIV)
> For it is by grace you have been saved, through faith—and this not from yourselves, it is the gift of God—not by works, so that no one can boast. *For we are God's workmanship, created in Christ Jesus to do good works, which God prepared in advance for us to do.*

Most are familiar with verses 8 and 9, but reread verse 10, the italicized last sentence. God has a plan for your life! There are some things that He wants you to accomplish!

Ephesians 4:11-13 (NIV)
> It was he who gave some to be apostles, some to be prophets, some to be evangelists, and some to be pastors and teachers, to prepare God's people for works of service, *so that the body of Christ may be built up until we all reach unity in the faith and in the knowledge of the Son of God and become mature, attaining to the whole measure of the fullness of Christ.*

What will your "good works" be shown for? Have you been building on your "foundation" with gold, silver, and costly stones, or wood, hay, and straw? Reread 1 Corinthians 3:10-15 again. Our works will be tested by fire and judged accordingly. What about my sins—all the "bad" stuff? Don't ever forget, *your sins are gone*. God has forgotten them—the precious blood of Jesus Christ has washed your sins away. Our rewards are based only upon the good things that we've accomplished for Christ while on this earth.

2 Corinthians 5:1-10 (NIV)
Now we know that if the earthly tent we live in is destroyed, we have a building from God, an eternal house in heaven, not built by human hands. Meanwhile we groan, longing to be clothed with our heavenly dwelling, because when we are clothed, we will not be found naked. For while we are in this tent, we groan and are burdened, because we do not wish to be unclothed but to be clothed with our heavenly dwelling, so that what is mortal may be swallowed up by life. Now it is God who has made us for this very purpose and has given us the Spirit as a deposit, guaranteeing what is to come. Therefore we are always confident and know that as long as we are at home in the body we are away from the Lord. We live by faith, not by sight. We are confident, I say, and would prefer to be away from the body and at home with the Lord. So we make it our goal to please him, whether we are at home in the body or away from it. *For we must all appear before the judgment seat of Christ, that each one may receive what is due him for the things done while in the body, whether good or bad.*

Will anyone receive judgment for their sins? Only those who have rejected God's free "gift" of salvation will receive penalty for their sin. God will judge every "unbeliever" *fairly*—based on how they lived their life. Remember, Jesus died for the sins of the whole world. The only sin that will ever send anyone to Hell is the *rejection* of Jesus Christ and His free *pardon* for all of our sins. No one will go to Hell because of any other sin. But wait, if you do reject this free "gift", then you will be judged *fairly* based on how you lived your life on earth—good deeds, bad deeds. Let's not "sugarcoat" it—Hell is still Hell, it's real and it involves separation from God for all eternity. Whose choice? Your choice!

Hebrews 2:1-3a (NIV)
We must pay more careful attention, therefore, to what we have heard, so that we do not drift away. For if the message spoken by angels was binding, and every violation and disobedience received its just punishment, *how shall we escape if we ignore such a great salvation?*

Let's talk more about this "faith" versus "works" issue.

James 2:14-24 (NIV)
What good is it, my brothers, if a man claims to have faith but has no deeds? Can such faith save him? Suppose a brother or sister is without clothes and daily food. If one of you says to him, "Go, I wish you well; keep warm and well fed," but does nothing about his physical needs, what good is it? In the same way, faith by itself, if it is not accompanied by action, is dead. But someone will say, "You have faith; I have deeds." Show me your faith without deeds, and I will show you my faith by what I do. You believe that there is one God.

Good! Even the demons believe that—and shudder. You foolish man, do you want evidence that faith without deeds is useless? Was not our ancestor Abraham considered righteous for what he did when he offered his son Isaac on the altar? You see that his faith and his actions were working together, and his faith was made complete by what he did. And the scripture was fulfilled that says, "Abraham believed God, and it was credited to him as righteousness," and he was called God's friend. *You see that a person is justified by what he does and not by faith alone.*

I know what you're saying—this doesn't make sense. James seems to be saying that we're justified by our "deeds?" Many fail to understand the point that James is trying to make. We are, indeed, made righteous by our faith *alone*. But, if our faith is genuine, it will by *natural progression* lead to "good works." What James is trying to say is that anyone who has a genuine, "saving" faith will, by their "new nature", be prompted on to good works (obedience). Abraham was "justified by faith"—he believed God and it was "credited to him as righteousness." Then what? This faith produced works. Abraham wasn't declared righteous by his *willingness* to sacrifice his son Isaac. His faith provided the willingness, which led to obedience. Abraham had been declared righteous *before* he actually placed Isaac on the altar. His faith, however, led to his willingness to be obedient to God.

I believe another classic example of this principle has to do with water baptism. We accept God's "gift" of salvation *by faith*, and this prompts us on to water baptism. It's an act of obedience to Christ –it's symbolic. If you fail to follow the natural progression, it's meaningless. If you have been baptized and/or confirmed (human works) apart from faith it means nothing. The faith always comes first! Don't forget the story that we discussed earlier in the book about the "thief on the cross." He demonstrated faith—received his salvation—then died and went to Heaven. He wasn't able to get any "good works" done to *finalize* his salvation—it was *complete* on the basis of *faith alone*!

1 Thessalonians 1:2-3 (NIV)
We always thank God for all of you, mentioning you in our prayers. We continually remember before our God and Father *your work produced by faith, your labor prompted by love, and your endurance inspired by h*ope in our Lord Jesus Christ.

"Work produced by faith, labor prompted by love, any endurance inspired by hope." The apostles asked Jesus the following question:

John 6:28-29 (NIV)
Then they asked him, "What must we do to do the works God requires?" Jesus answered, "The work of God is this: to believe in the one he has sent."

Jesus, Himself, said that "the work of God" would come as a result of *faith*—believe in the one He has sent. This was the place to start.

2 Corinthians 13:5-6 (NIV)
Examine yourselves to see whether you are in the faith; test yourselves. Do you not realize that Christ Jesus is in you—unless, of course, you fail the test? And I trust that you will discover that we have not failed the test.

Our *priority* should always be to focus on our relationship with God, through Jesus Christ. Then all of the other "good stuff"—the "fruit of the Spirit" (love, joy, peace, patience, kindness, goodness, faithfulness, gentleness and self-control) will be a by-product of this relationship. Always be mindful, however, that good deeds, hard work, and perseverance, by themselves, mean little. Look at what Jesus told this "church":

Revelation 2:2-5 (NIV)
I know your deeds, your hard work and your perseverance. I know that you cannot tolerate wicked men, that you have tested those who claim to be apostles but are not, and have found them false. You have persevered and have endured hardships for my name, and have not grown weary. *Yet I hold this against you: You have forsaken your first love.* Remember the height from which you have fallen! Repent and do the things you did at first. If you do not repent, I will come to you and remove your lampstand from its place.

They were doing some "good" things. What was wrong with that? They had the *order* all wrong—the relationship is to be the priority! Don't be a Martha—be a Mary!

Luke 10:38-42 (NIV)
As Jesus and his disciples were on their way, he came to a village where a woman named Martha opened her home to him. She had a sister called Mary, who sat at the Lord's feet listening to what he said. But Martha was distracted by all the preparations that had to be made. She came to him and asked, "Lord, don't you care that my sister has left me to do the work by myself? Tell her to help

me!" "Martha, Martha," the Lord answered, "you are worried and upset about many things, but only one thing is needed. Mary has chosen what is better, and it will not be taken away from her."

Mary had the proper perspective! Let your "good works" flow from a heart that is fixed on Jesus Christ. Let Him give you a "servant heart." Being a "servant" was very important in Jesus' economy. Look at what he said.

Mark 9:35 (NIV)
Sitting down, Jesus called the Twelve and said, "If anyone wants to be first, he must be the very last, and the servant of all."

Matthew 23:11-12 (NIV)
The greatest among you will be your servant. For whoever exalts himself will be humbled, and whoever humbles himself will be exalted.

Now look at what he did.

John 13:2-17 (NIV)
The evening meal was being served, and the devil had already prompted Judas Iscariot, son of Simon, to betray Jesus. Jesus knew that the Father had put all things under his power, and that he had come from God and was returning to God; so he got up from the meal, took off his outer clothing, and wrapped a towel around his waist. After that, he poured water into a basin and began to wash his disciples' feet, drying them with the towel that was wrapped around him. He came to Simon Peter, who said to him, "Lord, are you going to wash my feet?" Jesus replied, "You do not realize now what

I am doing, but later you will understand." "No," said Peter, "you shall never wash my feet." Jesus answered, "Unless I wash you, you have no part with me." "Then, Lord," Simon Peter replied, "not just my feet but my hands and my head as well!" Jesus answered, "A person who has had a bath needs only to wash his feet; his whole body is clean. And you are clean, though not every one of you." For he knew who was going to betray him, and that was why he said not every one was clean. When he had finished washing their feet, he put on his clothes and returned to his place. "Do you understand what I have done for you?" he asked them. "You call me 'Teacher' and 'Lord,' and rightly so, for that is what I am. Now that I, your Lord and Teacher, have washed your feet, you also should wash one another's feet. I have set you an example that you should do as I have done for you. I tell you the truth, no servant is greater than his master, nor is a messenger greater than the one who sent him. Now that you know these things, you will be blessed if you do them.

We've seen the same theme over and over again; our ability to do the "right" thing needs to come from God. We are not to do it in our own power and strength!

Galatians 3:3 (NIV)
Are you so foolish? After beginning with the Spirit, are you now trying to attain your goal by human effort?

Jude 24-25 (NIV)
To him who is able to keep you from falling and to present you before his glorious presence without

fault and with great joy—to the only God our Savior be glory, majesty, power and authority, through Jesus Christ our Lord, before all ages, now and forevermore! Amen.

1 Thessalonians 5:23-24 (NIV)
May God himself, the God of peace, sanctify you through and through. May your whole spirit, soul and body be kept blameless at the coming of our Lord Jesus Christ. *The one who calls you is faithful and he will do it.*

He will keep you from falling. He is "faithful!" It's all about the proper progression. Faith is what makes us "righteous" before God. Faith involves, first of all, hearing the word of God (i.e. attaining wisdom and knowledge). After hearing, we then believe and receive it, and, finally, we trust Him to bring it to pass. This faith will ultimately produce "good works", *if it is genuine.* Humble yourself before God, hunger for Him, and pursue Him with all of your might. Enter into His "workshop" with thanksgiving and praise, practice the "disciplines" and let God's Spirit empower you to bring forth "fruit" in your life. Do it all out of love for Him! This is how we can "grow in the grace in knowledge of our Lord and Savior Jesus Christ."

1 Peter 1:3-9 (NIV)
Praise be to the God and Father of our Lord Jesus Christ! In his great mercy he has given us new birth into a living hope through the resurrection of Jesus Christ from the dead, and into an inheritance that can never perish, spoil or fade—kept in heaven for you, who through faith are shielded by God's power until the coming of the salvation that is ready to be revealed in the last time. In this you

greatly rejoice, though now for a little while you may have had to suffer grief in all kinds of trials. These have come so that your faith—of greater worth than gold, which perishes even though refined by fire—may be proved genuine and may result in praise, glory and honor when Jesus Christ is revealed. Though you have not seen him, you love him; and even though you do not see him now, you believe in him and are filled with an inexpressible and glorious joy, for you are receiving the goal of your faith, the salvation of your souls.

How do Christians "fall away" or "wander" from their faith? Another favorite term is "backsliding." I know that I feel like a "specialist" when it comes to this one! I've spent a number of years trying to figure out how to get back on the racecourse. Even when I'd get back into the "race", I just couldn't seem to "get going!" Can anyone relate? What does cause us to stumble, and fall, in our "race?" Can you lose your salvation? This is another issue that has caused divisions in the Church. I believe that there are three circumstances that caused "believers" to "fall away."

- We are primarily influenced by our own "sin nature" which still lives within us (remember that it's constantly battling with our "new nature")
- We can be negatively influenced by Satan and his demons (this is oppression—not possession)
- We can be negatively influenced by other human beings (which is indirectly from Satan himself)

I started with the most common one first. Our "sin nature" rearing it's ugly head!

James 1:13-15 (NIV)
> When tempted, no one should say, "God is tempting me." For God cannot be tempted by evil, nor does he tempt anyone; but each one is tempted when, *by his own evil desire*, he is dragged away and enticed. Then, after desire has conceived, it gives birth to sin; and sin, when it is full-grown, gives birth to death.

We are instructed to "throw off everything that hinders and the sin that so easily entangles." Easier said than done, you say?

Hebrews 12:1-3 (NIV)
> Therefore, since we are surrounded by such a great cloud of witnesses, *let us throw off everything that hinders and the sin that so easily entangles*, and let us run with perseverance the race marked out for us. Let us fix our eyes on Jesus, the author and perfecter of our faith, who for the joy set before him endured the cross, scorning its shame, and sat down at the right hand of the throne of God. Consider him who endured such opposition from sinful men, so that you will not grow weary and lose heart.

Do Christian's sin? I think you already know the answer to that one—of course we do. How does "sinning" cause problems for the Christian? It breaks our *fellowship* with God. I have been "born-again" for over 25 years, in spite of that I know that some of my most grievous sins occurred after I was saved! Did I lose my salvation? Absolutely not! There was, however, a price. It hurt my *relationship* with God. It affected my ability to have *fellowship* with God. Did God stop loving me? Not for a second. Did God allow things to happen in my life to gently (sometimes not so gently) restore my relationship with Him? Yes. Remember, *God never turns His back on us—we turn our backs on Him.* God will always love us and nothing can separate us from that love.

Romans 8:31-39 (NIV)
What, then, shall we say in response to this? If God is for us, who can be against us? He who did not spare his own Son, but gave him up for us all—how will he not also, along with him, graciously give us all things? Who will bring any charge against those whom God has chosen? It is God who justifies. Who is he that condemns? Christ Jesus, who died—more than that, who was raised to life—is at the right hand of God and is also interceding for us. Who shall separate us from the love of Christ? Shall trouble or hardship or persecution or famine or nakedness or danger or sword? As it is written: "For your sake we face death all day long; we are considered as sheep to be slaughtered."

No, in all these things we are more than conquerors through him who loved us. *For I am convinced that neither death nor life, neither angels nor demons, neither the present nor the future, nor any powers, neither height nor depth, nor anything else in all creation, will be able to separate us from the love of God that is in Christ Jesus our Lord.*

We have a promise from God that we will not be tempted beyond what we're able to endure.

1 Corinthians 10:13 (NIV)
No temptation has seized you except what is common to man. And God is faithful; he will not let

you be tempted beyond what you can bear. But when you are tempted, he will also provide a way out so that you can stand up under it.

We also have promises that there is nothing that Satan, or any other human being, can do to separate us from God. Even though nothing can separate us from God's love, our fellowship with Him can still be broken by sin. Unfortunately, our "sin nature" can, and still does, cause problems. Remember, there is a war raging between the two "natures." How can you assure victory for your "new nature?" By living in, and by, the Spirit of Christ, which lives in you!

Lamentations 5:15-16 (NIV)
Joy is gone from our hearts; our dancing has turned to mourning. The crown has fallen from our head. Woe to us, for we have sinned!

Isaiah 59:2 (NIV)
But your iniquities have separated you from your God; your sins have hidden his face from you, so that he will not hear.

If you are a "believer", and you are caught up in a habitual sin, God will first cause a conviction in your Spirit and then, if you are willing, He will break the bonds that hold you and give you the power to overcome. We are instructed to confess the sin and repent (turn away).

1 John 1:8-9 (NIV)
If we claim to be without sin, we deceive ourselves and the truth is not in us. If we confess our sins, he is faithful and just and will forgive us our sins and purify us from all unrighteousness.

If God sees that it is truly our desire to stop sinning, He will provide the "cure." What happens if you *deliberately continue* in your sinning? If you willfully disobey, there will be *consequences* for your sin. This could lead to trials and sufferings—God's discipline. If you ignore God's discipline, and persist in your sin, the situation can begin to enter "dangerous territory." Many believe that once you experience the" instantaneous transformation" you can never lose your salvation. I believe that *practically speaking* this is true, but I still believe that you can "give away" your salvation. I know many will disagree with this perspective, but I think that God's word is clear that it can happen. Is it a common occurrence? Absolutely not!

If you make a legitimate decision to accept God's "gift" of forgiveness and accept the "righteousness" that Christ provides, you do not all of a sudden turn into a robot without free will. God doesn't change us into robots! You can still, at any time, make a choice to reject Christ. The real issue is will you want to. The danger lies in persisting in your sin—this can cause a "hardening" of your heart, which could lead you, ultimately, to renouncing Christ. You then, *in your own free will*, decide that you really don't believe that Christ did what He said He did. If you genuinely accept, then reject God's "gift", this can, according to Scripture, lead to the "giving away" (loss) of your salvation.

Hebrews 6:4-12 (NIV)

> It is impossible for those who have once been enlightened, who have tasted the heavenly gift, who have shared in the Holy Spirit, who have tasted the goodness of the word of God and the powers of the coming age, if they fall away, to be brought back to repentance, because to their loss they are crucifying the Son of God all over again and subjecting him to public disgrace. Land that

drinks in the rain often falling on it and that produces a crop useful to those for whom it is farmed receives the blessing of God. But land that produces thorns and thistles is worthless and is in danger of being cursed. In the end it will be burned. Even though we speak like this, dear friends, we are confident of better things in your case—things that accompany salvation. God is not unjust; he will not forget your work and the love you have shown him as you have helped his people and continue to help them. We want each of you to show this same diligence to the very end, in order to make your hope sure. We do not want you to become lazy, but to imitate those who through faith and patience inherit what has been promised.

You cannot explain this verse away. I believe, however, that this is not a frequent event. If you are even concerned about whether or not this applies to you then I can guarantee that you are still okay with God—you still have a sensitive Spirit. God will not let you go without a fight! The danger lies in *willful, persistent, deliberate disobedience* to God.

Hebrews 10:26-31 (NIV)
If we deliberately keep on sinning after we have received the knowledge of the truth, no sacrifice for sins is left, but only a fearful expectation of judgment and of raging fire that will consume the enemies of God. Anyone who rejected the law of Moses died without mercy on the testimony of two or three witnesses. How much more severely do you think a man deserves to be punished who has trampled the Son of God under foot, who has treated as an unholy thing the blood of the

covenant that sanctified him, and who has insulted the Spirit of grace? For we know him who said, "It is mine to avenge; I will repay," and again, "The Lord will judge his people." It is a dreadful thing to fall into the hands of the living God.

2 Peter 2:20-22 (NIV)
If they have escaped the corruption of the world by knowing our Lord and Savior Jesus Christ and are again entangled in it and overcome, they are worse off at the end than they were at the beginning. It would have been better for them not to have known the way of righteousness, than to have known it and then to turn their backs on the sacred command that was passed on to them. Of them the proverbs are true: "A dog returns to its vomit," and, "A sow that is washed goes back to her wallowing in the mud."

We now understand that it is *sin* that caused barriers between God and us. Jesus Christ broke down the barriers. Sin, however, can continue to cause problems in our lives, if we allow it to—especially willful, persistent, deliberate sinning. Remember, however, there are certain sins, addictions, and other problems, that can take years to overcome, *even in God's power*. What about all the sin's that we commit as Christians every day—some that we don't even realize? Remember, if you are a "believer", they are *all gone*. God has forgotten them. You say, "It doesn't make sense—how can it be?" It's all about grace! God's grace—unmerited favor—makes up the difference. Grace covers it all! Remember, God is looking at your heart. Just continue to "run the race" and *let Him empower you to change*. It may seem like slow progress but He is faithful!

2 Peter 1:3-4 (NIV)
His divine power has given us everything we need for life and godliness through our knowledge of him who called us by his own glory and goodness. Through these he has given us his very great and precious promises, so that through them you may participate in the divine nature and escape the corruption in the world caused by evil desires

Ephesians 3:7 (NIV)
I became a servant of this gospel by the gift of God's grace given me through the working of his power.

How does God instruct us to deal with Satan? His word says to "resist the devil and he will flee from you."

James 4:7-8 (NIV)
Submit yourselves, then, to God. Resist the devil, and he will flee from you. Come near to God and he will come near to you. Wash your hands, you sinners, and purify your hearts, you double-minded.

Use God's armor as we discussed in the last chapter. Avoid evil and anything that could cause you to "wander from the faith." What else can cause us to "fall away?" The influence of "unbelievers."

2 Peter 3:17-18 (NIV)
Therefore, dear friends, since you already know this, be on your guard so that you may not be carried away by the error of lawless men and fall from your secure position. But grow in the grace and knowledge of our Lord and Savior Jesus Christ. To him be glory both now and forever! Amen.

We're instructed to avoid "being carried away by the error of lawless men." We should avoid spending excessive time with "unbelievers." We are instructed to be in the world, but not of the world. Look at what Jesus said just before he ascended into Heaven.

John 17:13-18 (NIV)
"I am coming to you now, but I say these things while I am still in the world, so that they may have the full measure of my joy within them. I have given them your word and the world has hated them, for they are not of the world any more than I am of the world. My prayer is not that you take them out of the world but that you protect them from the evil one. They are not of the world, even as I am not of it. Sanctify them by the truth; your word is truth. As you sent me into the world, I have sent them into the world.

You'll be influenced in a negative way if all of your friends and companions are "nonbelievers." Their sinful lifestyles can "rub-off" onto you.

1 Corinthians 15:33 (NIV)
Do not be misled: "Bad company corrupts good character."

Peer pressure is a powerful force. Spend plenty of time with God's people—people who love Christ—and they will "infect" you in a positive way. This, however, doesn't mean that we shouldn't spend time with "unbelievers." Remember, Jesus commonly ate with the "tax collectors and sinners"—He didn't, however, let them influence Him, He influenced them! It's important that we "let our light shine" before all men, but be careful not to get tangled up in their "web!" Understand that sin is like a cancer that requires a radical surgery. Paul talked about "putting out of your fellowship" the person who is caught up in sin.

1 Corinthians 5:1-5 (NIV)
It is actually reported that there is sexual immorality among you, and of a kind that does not occur even among pagans: A man has his father's wife. And you are proud! Shouldn't you rather have been filled with grief and have put out of your fellowship the man who did this? Even though I am not physically present, I am with you in spirit. And I have already passed judgment on the one who did this, just as if I were present. When you are assembled in the name of our Lord Jesus and I am with you in spirit, and the power of our Lord Jesus is present, hand this man over to Satan, so that the sinful nature may be destroyed and his spirit saved on the day of the Lord.

He even stresses the importance of confronting, in a loving way the brother, or sister, in Christ who is caught up in sin.

2 Thessalonians 3:6, 14-16 (NIV)
In the name of the Lord Jesus Christ, we command you, brothers, to keep away from every brother who is idle and does not live according to the teaching you received from us.....If anyone does not obey our instruction in this letter, take special note of him. Do not associate with him, in order that he may feel ashamed. Yet do not regard him as an enemy, but warn him as a brother.

Galatians 6:1 (NIV)
Brothers, if someone is caught in a sin, you who are spiritual should restore him gently. But watch yourself, or you also may be tempted.

Sin works like this in our lives as well. We do need to have *zero tolerance* for "sin", but never forget that we do have to separate the "sin" from the "sinner!" God hates the "sin", but God loves the "sinner." Christ gave His life for you while you were still a "sinner."

Romans 5:8 (NIV)
But God demonstrates his own love for us in this: While we were still sinners, Christ died for us.

How can we love our enemies, or anyone else who has hurt us? How can we separate the "sin" from the "sinner?" Who is it that changes a heart? That's right, *only God can transform us from the inside-out and bring about real, lasting changes*. Once we understand that *real change* is a "God-thing", then we can take a breather from our futile efforts of trying to control, manipulate, and change people. Just love them and let God do the changing! Just be wary of this sin—it can be subtle and enticing. Don't give it a foothold. One habitual sin can quickly spread into every other area of your life—like a cancer.

Sinning, not only breaks fellowship with God, it can "grieve" the Holy Spirit living inside of you.

Ephesians 4:30 (NIV)
And do not grieve the Holy Spirit of God, with whom you were sealed for the day of redemption.

God lights a "pilot light" within us at the "instantaneous transformation." This is the presence of the Holy Spirit. The "pilot light" can be the source of a mighty flame *if you allow God to do it.*

2 Timothy 1:6-7 (NIV)
For this reason I remind you to fan into flame the gift of God, which is in you through the laying on of my hands. For God did not give us a spirit of timidity, but a spirit of power, of love and of self-discipline.

Sin and disobedience will hinder your spiritual growth more than anything else. It'll cause you to go from running to walking, and then, eventually to crawling. Don't let it cause you to stop the race! Confess your sin to God and repent. Turn away from your sin. Understand that it is like a dangerously spreading cancer that will overtake you if you don't allow God to perform surgery. Let God know that you are "powerless" to quit. What then? Into His "workshop", practice the "disciplines", be patient, and trust God. This is where you'll get the power to stop sinning. The changes may likely take time. Remember, above all, God's grace will make up for any shortcomings.

Titus 2:11-14 (NIV)
For the grace of God that brings salvation has appeared to all men. It teaches us to say "No" to ungodliness and worldly passions, and to live self-controlled, upright and godly lives in this present age, while we wait for the blessed hope—the glorious appearing of our great God and Savior, Jesus Christ, who gave himself for us to redeem us from all wickedness and to purify for himself a people that are his very own, eager to do what is good.

What should our goal be? It should be to *increase our faith* so that we can "say 'No' to ungodliness and worldly passions, and to live self-controlled, upright and godly lives in this present age." What is "faith?" How can we cause it to increase?

Hebrews 11:1 (NIV)
Now faith is being sure of what we hope for and certain of what we do not see.

"Faith" is really a *fusion* of the following three things:

- To gain wisdom and knowledge (God's word—interpreted by His Spirit)
- To believe, and receive, this newly found wisdom and knowledge
- To trust and obey God

Isaiah 33:6 (NIV)
He will be the sure foundation for your times, a rich store of salvation and wisdom and knowledge; *the fear of the LORD is the key to this treasure.*

The key to the treasure is the "fear of the Lord!" What does it mean to "fear the Lord?" This isn't a popular notion in our culture. Everyone wants to focus solely on God's love, but remember there are many other facets to God's character. What do I mean by " Godly fear?" It should be a *balance* between dread/terror and awe/reverence.

Dread and terror cause us to want to *run away*—to be afraid and to hide our faces.

Isaiah 8:13 (NIV)
The LORD Almighty is the one you are to regard as holy, he is the one you are to fear, he is the one you are to dread…

Exodus 20:18-21 (NIV)

When the people saw the thunder and lightning and heard the trumpet and saw the mountain in smoke, they trembled with fear. They stayed at a distance and said to Moses, "Speak to us yourself and we will listen. But do not have God speak to us or we will die." Moses said to the people, "Do not be afraid. God has come to test you, so that the fear of God will be with you to keep you from sinning." The people remained at a distance, while Moses approached the thick darkness where God was.

Matthew 10:28 (NIV)

Do not be afraid of those who kill the body but cannot kill the soul. Rather, be afraid of the One who can destroy both soul and body in hell.

Reverence and awe, however, *draw us to Him*—His glory, His Majesty, His wondrous love.

1 Chronicles 29:11 (NIV)

Yours, O LORD, is the greatness and the power and the glory and the majesty and the splendor, for everything in heaven and earth is yours. Yours, O LORD, is the kingdom; you are exalted as head over all.

1 John 4:16-19 (NIV)

And so we know and rely on the love God has for us. God is love. Whoever lives in love lives in God, and God in him. In this way, love is made complete among us so that we will have confidence on the day of judgment, because in this world we are like him. There is no fear in love. But perfect love drives out fear, because fear has to do with punishment. The one who fears is not made perfect in love. We love because he first loved us.

Hebrews 12:28-29(NIV)
Therefore, since we are receiving a kingdom that cannot be shaken, let us be thankful, and so worship God acceptably with reverence and awe, for our "God is a consuming fire."

Yes, we are drawn to the fire, but be careful because fire can cause you harm if you don't respect it! Fire is "light" and the light captivates us. Who is the "light?"

John 8:12 (NIV)
When Jesus spoke again to the people, he said, "I am the light of the world. Whoever follows me will never walk in darkness, but will have the light of life."

We need to strike a proper balance between "dread/terror" and "awe/reverence." Can't I just love God? By all means, but if you *fear God* it gives you a willingness to do what God says. This will allow you to express to God *practical love*—love that drives us to *willing obedience*.

John 14:15 (NIV)
"If you love me, you will obey what I command.

To "fear the Lord" is to have a *sure foundation* for salvation, wisdom, and knowledge. Once the foundation has been established, it can be built upon. It's best to build upon a stable foundation. Rock works the best! Jesus Christ is the rock!

Matthew 7:24-27 (NIV)
"Therefore everyone who hears these words of mine and puts them into practice is like a wise man who built his house on the rock. The rain came down, the streams rose, and the winds blew and beat against that house; yet it did not fall, because it had its foundation on the rock. But everyone who hears these words of mine and does not put them into practice is like a foolish man who built his house on sand. The rain came down, the streams rose, and the winds blew and beat against that house, and it fell with a great crash."

Romans 9:33 (NIV)
As it is written: "See, I lay in Zion a stone that causes men to stumble and a rock that makes them fall, and the one who trusts in him will never be put to shame."

After we have established our *sure* foundation by understanding the "fear of the Lord", how do we start to build upon it? What is the first step in the building of our faith?

Romans 10:17 (NIV)
Consequently, faith comes from hearing the message, and the message is heard through the word of Christ.

After we "hear" (acquire the wisdom and knowledge), we believe, and receive it as our own. This involves the practical application of God's wisdom and knowledge—obedience. Then, all that's left is to trust God to bring it to pass. This "trust" is the completion of our faith! It all starts, however, with obtaining God's wisdom and knowledge!

Psalm 111:10 (NIV)
The fear of the L ORD is the beginning of wisdom; all who follow his precepts have good understanding. To him belongs eternal praise.

Proverbs 2:1-6 (NIV)
My son, if you accept my words and store up my commands within you, turning your ear to wisdom and applying your heart to understanding, and if you call out for insight and cry aloud for understanding, and if you look for it as for silver and search for it as for hidden treasure, then you will understand the fear of the L ORD and find the knowledge of God. For the L ORD gives wisdom, and from his mouth come knowledge and understanding.

James 3:17 (NIV)
But the wisdom that comes from heaven is first of all pure; then peace-loving, considerate, submissive, full of mercy and good fruit, impartial and sincere.

Romans 11:33-34 (NIV)
Oh, the depth of the riches of the wisdom and knowledge of God! How unsearchable his judgments, and his paths beyond tracing out! "Who has known the mind of the Lord? Or who has been his counselor?"

How can we get God's wisdom and knowledge? James makes it very clear that we are, first of all to ask God for it, and then believe that we will get it!

James 1:5-7 (NIV)
If any of you lacks wisdom, he should ask God,

who gives generously to all without finding fault, and it will be given to him. But when he asks, he must believe and not doubt, because he who doubts is like a wave of the sea, blown and tossed by the wind. That man should not think he will receive anything from the Lord.

Solomon had much to say about wisdom and knowledge. How did he get so wise? He asked God for it!

2 Chronicles 1:7-12 (NIV)
That night God appeared to Solomon and said to him, "Ask for whatever you want me to give you." Solomon answered God, "You have shown great kindness to David my father and have made me king in his place. Now, LORD God, let your promise to my father David be confirmed, for you have made me king over a people who are as numerous as the dust of the earth. Give me wisdom and knowledge, that I may lead this people, for who is able to govern this great people of yours?" God said to Solomon, "Since this is your heart's desire and you have not asked for wealth, riches or honor, nor for the death of your enemies, and since you have not asked for a long life but for wisdom and knowledge to govern my people over whom I have made you king, therefore wisdom and knowledge will be given you. And I will also give you wealth, riches and honor, such as no king who was before you ever had and none after you will have."

2 Chronicles 9:22-23 (NIV)
King Solomon was greater in riches and wisdom than all the other kings of the earth. All the kings

of the earth sought audience with Solomon to hear the wisdom God had put in his heart.

After you've asked, and believe, God will begin to supply the wisdom and knowledge—via His word, and by His Spirit. It can come in many different ways: your own reading, meditating, and studying of the scriptures, or through other believers (pastors, teachers, etc.). God's Word, however, is the key.

> **2 Timothy 3:14-15 (NIV)**
> But as for you, continue in what you have learned and have become convinced of, because you know those from whom you learned it, and how from infancy you have *known the holy Scriptures, which are able to make you wise for salvation through faith in Christ Jesus.*

It will require *discipline* as we've already discussed. You have to enter into His "workshop!"
Who holds the key to all wisdom and knowledge? Jesus Christ!

> **Colossians 2:2-3 (NIV)**
> My purpose is that they may be encouraged in heart and united in love, so that they may have the full riches of complete understanding, in order that they may know the mystery of God, namely, Christ, *in whom are hidden all the treasures of wisdom and knowledge.*

> **Ephesians 3:7-12 (NIV)**
> I became a servant of this gospel by the gift of God's grace given me through the working of his power. Although I am less than the least of all

God's people, this grace was given me: to preach to the Gentiles *the unsearchable riches of Christ*, and to make plain to everyone the administration of this mystery, which for ages past was kept hidden in God, who created all things. His intent was that now, through the church, the manifold wisdom of God should be made known to the rulers and authorities in the heavenly realms, according to his eternal purpose which he accomplished in Christ Jesus our Lord. In him and through faith in him we may approach God with freedom and confidence.

Never forget, however, that God's wisdom is different from man's wisdom.

Isaiah 2:22 (NIV)
Stop trusting in man, who has but a breath in his nostrils. Of what account is he?

1 Corinthians 3:18-20 (NIV)
Do not deceive yourselves. If any one of you thinks he is wise by the standards of this age, he should become a "fool" so that he may become wise. For the wisdom of this world is foolishness in God's sight. As it is written: "He catches the wise in their craftiness"; and again, "The Lord knows that the thoughts of the wise are futile."

1 Corinthians 1:17-31 (NIV)
For Christ did not send me to baptize, but to preach the gospel—not with words of human wisdom, lest the cross of Christ be emptied of its power. For the message of the cross is foolishness to those who

are perishing, but to us who are being saved it is the power of God. For it is written: "I will destroy the wisdom of the wise; the intelligence of the intelligent I will frustrate."Where is the wise man? Where is the scholar? Where is the philosopher of this age? Has not God made foolish the wisdom of the world? For since in the wisdom of God the world through its wisdom did not know him, God was pleased through the foolishness of what was preached to save those who believe. Jews demand miraculous signs and Greeks look for wisdom, but we preach Christ crucified: a stumbling block to Jews and foolishness to Gentiles, but to those whom God has called, both Jews and Greeks, Christ the power of God and the wisdom of God. For the foolishness of God is wiser than man's wisdom, and the weakness of God is stronger than man's strength. Brothers, think of what you were when you were called. Not many of you were wise by human standards; not many were influential; not many were of noble birth. But God chose the foolish things of the world to shame the wise; God chose the weak things of the world to shame the strong. He chose the lowly things of this world and the despised things—and the things that are not—to nullify the things that are, so that no one may boast before him. It is because of him that you are in Christ Jesus, who has become for us wisdom from God—that is, our righteousness, holiness and redemption. Therefore, as it is written: "Let him who boasts boast in the Lord."

God's wisdom can ultimately lead to perfection. The apostle Paul said it best.

A Prescription for the Impotent Christian

Colossians 1:28-29 (NIV)
We proclaim him, admonishing and teaching everyone with all wisdom, so that we may present everyone perfect in Christ. To this end I labor, struggling with all his energy, which so powerfully works in me.

Notice the last sentence; Paul struggled with *all of God's energy* not his own. God gave him wisdom and Paul not only applied it to his own life, but also taught it to others. Many have heard about the "Prayer of Jabez", but I would like to more closely examine what I call the "Prayer of Paul." How many of the following would you like to have in your life?

1. To live a life worthy of the Lord—*to please Him in every way.*
2. To bear fruit in *every* good work.
3. To grow in the knowledge of God.
4. To be strengthened with all power according to His glorious might.
5. To have great endurance, patience, in "running your race."

Wow! It sounds like a perfect "wish list" for the Christian. What *did* Paul pray for?

Colossians 1:9-14(NIV)
For this reason, since the day we heard about you, we have not stopped praying for you and *asking God to fill you with the knowledge of his will through all spiritual wisdom and understanding.* And we pray this in order that you may live a life worthy of the Lord and may please him in every way: bearing fruit in every good work, growing in the knowledge of God, being strengthened with all

power according to his glorious might so that you may have great endurance and patience, and joyfully giving thanks to the Father, who has qualified you to share in the inheritance of the saints in the kingdom of light. For he has rescued us from the dominion of darkness and brought us into the kingdom of the Son he loves, in whom we have redemption, the forgiveness of sins.

Paul asked God to "fill them with the knowledge of His will through all spiritual wisdom and understanding." If you pray this to God, then the list above will be yours. What is God's desire for your life? He has chosen you since the "beginning" of the world.

2 Thessalonians 2:13-15 (NIV)
But we ought always to thank God for you, brothers loved by the Lord, because *from the beginning God chose you* to be saved through the sanctifying work of the Spirit and through belief in the truth. He called you to this through our gospel, that you might share in the glory of our Lord Jesus Christ. So then, brothers, stand firm and hold to the teachings we passed on to you, whether by word of mouth or by letter.

He has a purpose and destiny for your life. He broke down all the barriers that separated us from Him. He lives inside of every Christian that has been "spiritually" reborn. This Spirit is available to help us "run our race." We need only to seek Him diligently by entering into His "workshop", humbly, hungry, and holy. Give Him the thanksgiving and praise He deserves. Begin to practice the "spiritual and physical disciplines" and understand that trials and suffering increase our faith and perseverance. If you should stumble (or fall) that's OK. God's grace will pick you up and dust you off. He'll even carry you if you need it! Confess your sin and move on. Trust that God will ultimately bring forth victory. Never forget that God is faithful and He will do it. Seek God's wisdom and apply it to your life. Ask to "be filled with the knowledge of his will through all spiritual wisdom and understanding." Trust and obey His words—they will bring perfect peace, joy, and happiness. If we could only grasp the incredible love that God has for us!

Ephesians 3:16-19 (NIV)
> I pray that out of his glorious riches he may strengthen you with power through his Spirit in your inner being, so that Christ may dwell in your hearts through faith. And I pray that you, being rooted and established in love, may have power, together with all the saints, *to grasp how wide and long and high and deep is the love of Christ, and to know this love that surpasses knowledge*—that you may be filled to the measure of all the fullness of God.

It is my prayer that God will allow you to taste of this unfathomable love—it will change you forever!

Now what? If you've never experienced the "instantaneous transformation" that we talked about in the beginning you do not have a foundation to build upon. Please reread it if you must.

2 Corinthians 6:2 (NIV)
> For he says, "In the time of my favor I heard you, and in the day of salvation I helped you."

I tell you, now is the time of God's favor, now is the day of salvation.

Am I Perfect Yet?

It is my hope that after you've made this decision that you can begin to experience "growth" in your Christian walk—no longer an ineffective, impotent Christian. You can "run the race" as God intended. There is a song that I believe summarizes my book very well. I'll end with the words to that song. God bless you.

I'm Waiting for You
Words & Music: **Michael W. Smith, David Mullen, and Sam Mullins**

I walked this road
So very long ago
To show the way
So you would know
I walked the road
With holes in my hands and feet
To make the way
Come follow me

Chorus:
No, you are not alone
You will be free indeed
The journey begins and ends
With me
One million miles
It starts with a step or two
What are you waiting for?
I'm waiting for you
You run the race
Thinking you've almost won
Then you may find
You've only begun
You're on the road

Thinking you're far from here
And suddenly find
You're very near

Chorus:
No, you are not alone
You will be free indeed
The journey begins and ends
With me
One million miles
It starts with a step or two
What are you waiting for?
I'm waiting for you

Printed in the United States
839400002B